The Principles and Practi

The Chartered Institute of Marketi

The Chartered Institute of Marketing was
founded in 1911. It is now the largest and
most successful marketing management
organisation in Europe with over 20,000
members and 16,000 students throughout
the world. The CIM is a democratic
organisation and is run for the members by
the members with the assistance of a
permanent staff headed by the Director
General. The Headquarters of CIM are at
Moor Hall, Cookham, near Maidenhead, in
Berkshire.

Objectives: The objectives of CIM are to
develop knowledge about marketing, to
provide services for members and registered
students and to make the principles and
practices of marketing more widely known
and used throughout industry and
commerce.

Range of activities: CIM's activities are
divided into four main areas:
    Membership and membership activities
    Corporate activities
    Marketing education
    Marketing training

BY THE SAME AUTHOR

Commercial Marketing
Commercial Merchandising

OTHER TITLES IN THE SERIES

The Principles and Practice of Selling

ALAN GILLAM
FCInstM, FRSA, MMRS, MIMC

Published on behalf of
the Chartered Institute of Marketing

Heinemann Professional Publishing

Heinemann Professional Publishing Ltd
Halley Court, Jordan Hill, Oxford OX2 8EJ

OXFORD   LONDON   MELBOURNE   AUCKLAND   SINGAPORE
IBADAN   NAIROBI   GABORONE   KINGSTON

First published 1982
Reprinted 1986, 1988, 1989 (twice)

ISBN 0 434 90661 1

Typeset by Robcroft Ltd, London WC1
Printed and bound in Great Britain by
Biddles Ltd, Guildford and King's Lynn

Preface

This book was written in response to a demand for an up-dated approach to the practice of selling.

Some of the principles of professional selling have remained unchanged, but it was considered that the place of selling within the modern concept of marketing and the application of those principles to changed market conditions needed to be emphasized.

The book sets out the role of selling within the modern marketing function as well as its relations with other functions of the enterprise. In addition, the practice of selling in the changed market conditions is explained.

The book is intended both as a guide to salesmen who wish to improve their performances and their earnings and as an aid to those responsible for training salesmen.

There is also a chapter on career prospects for salesmen.

N.B. The terms 'salesman' and 'he' are not intended to be exclusive but are used for simplicity's sake, to avoid the reiteration of 'salesman or saleswoman' and 'he or she' each time a practitioner of the profession is mentioned.

A.G.

Contents

Preface

1 The Salesman

The impetus behind the industrialization of the world economy undoubtedly came from the inventiveness of engineers. The development of the steam engine, mechanical processes of manufacture and other technological achievements burst upon the world in the nineteenth century just at a time when communications were improving and the developments could be exploited more rapidly.

The salesman played a minor role at this stage but, as processes developed, patents ran out and competition became more intense, there came a need for people skilled in the presentation of goods.

The presentation of goods or salesmanship is a highly skilled art but it is not one of those arts which is born in people. Proficiency in salesmanship, like most skills, can be acquired by the industry and application of the individual. Anyone of average intelligence and ability can learn the skills which are necessary to become proficient but, as in all other professions, above average intelligence and ability will produce a far better salesman or saleswoman.

The person who wishes to become an outstandingly good salesman must be prepared to make sacrifices of leisure time and other interests; he or she must be prepared to study and to work hard.

There is no absolute form of measurement for proficiency in selling. People's ability in this field cannot be compared as easily as material matters such as length, breadth or volume. For example, in law and accountancy there are definite right and wrong answers but in salesmanship the difference is one of degree or the difference between effective and less effective contact with the customer.

The difference between say, law and accountancy and selling is similar to the difference between a science and an art. Science deals with facts and progress is often a series of empirical judgments but art deals with opinion, taste and the personal response of the individual.

Success in artistic fields depends almost entirely on the degree of favourable response which the work of art evokes. Similarly, success in the field of selling depends upon the degree of favourable responses which the salesman gets from his customers.

Progress in salesmanship develops from practice and the intelligent application of experience. Unlike scientists the salesman is making decisions, based on his own judgments, at every call on every day. Each interview which a salesman conducts provides him with opportunities to exercise his skills and to develop his capacity.

The absence of absolute standards of measurement of salesmanship is one of the main reasons for the importance of training. Any training towards proficiency in salesmanship is largely a matter of self teaching by the individual. This book aims to set out the qualities and attributes which a salesman needs to reach a proficient standard and to show ways and means of acquiring these characteristics.

The book is intended to form the basis for study both for newcomers to the selling profession and for existing salesmen who may wish to improve their performance. It is hoped that in some cases, salesmen will have a better understanding of their role and function, that they will be able to improve both their performances and their incomes and with this better understanding, be encouraged to take the first steps towards sales and marketing management.

The structure of the book follows a logical sequence and deals with the three main parts of the selling process which are, the salesman, personal selling and managing the territory. These three parts are followed by two 'technical' chapters.

The first part, comprising Chapters I and II, concerns the role and function of the salesman, the relationship between his role and other functions within the enterprise, the desirable personal qualifications and, in the second chapter, product analysis and the development and preparation of selling points.

The next three chapters are concerned with the second part of the selling process and deal with personal selling. The pre-interview preparations are described and the structure of the sales interview is discussed. The two remaining chapters in this section of the selling process bring out the psychological aspects of selling and the techniques of overcoming objections.

The third part, spread over two chapters, goes into some detail regarding managing the territory, journey planning, profitability of the salesman, prospection, sales reports and finally record keeping.

The two 'technical' chapters discuss respectively the special problems of industrial selling and the career prospects open to salesmen.

It is believed that the book will form the basis from which a student can work and the bibliography should be read so that a broader field of knowledge can be explored. The book is also written with the wider purpose of setting out, in an easily accessible form, a body of knowledge which the practising salesman can consult. It is meant to be of practical benefit and to be used as a working handbook by both the student and the experienced representative. The saying 'One is never too old to learn' applies appropriately to the field of selling and the more capable and experienced salesmen are always the first to seek ways and means of extending their knowledge and capacities.

The degree to which the salesman can use the book to improve his own standards depends entirely upon the individual. Ultimately, each salesman has his future in his own hands and his success depends upon his intelligence, his industry and his determination.

Self-teaching imposes the hard control of self discipline and the single mindedness of determination. It is a hard road to follow but, to the successful man, the rewards can be rich in personal experience and material benefits. The men who succeed in selling are those with courage, high intelligence, personal integrity, personality, resourcefulness and determination. These are not ready-made qualities but ones which a man develops in himself from braving the adversities and accepting the successes of his life. They are qualities which a man creates in himself and are summed up in the word 'character'.

The book is designed to help salesmen by giving guidance but in the final resort it is the salesman's willingness to teach himself and consciously strive to exercise his skills that will improve the individual standards of performance.

The Salesman's Role and Function

In succeeding generations the salesman has become increasingly important as the vital link between the manufacturer and the distributor and user. The selling process is an esential part of the marketing mix. A well-organized company will have made a thorough marketing research, evolved a product policy and taken decisions on advertising, pricing, packaging, distribution channels and the calibre and size of the sales force. Each of these is an important ingredient and each plays its part.

However, the final link in the marketing chain is that of the salesman who makes the personal presentation of his company's goods or services.

Buyers can buy without a salesman being present but they tend to buy minimum quantities and to confine their orders to known lines. An interesting analysis of the sales records of a company revealed a sudden drop in sales when the sales force went on holiday during the first two weeks of August to coincide with the annual factory shut down. The product was a 'near monopoly' food and audits of stock levels in retail shops conducted at the same time showed a sharp increase in the out of stock position. There was a significant loss of sales solely through the absence of the salesmen; an example of the old saying 'out of sight out of mind'.

There has been a growing awareness of the increasing importance of the salesman as the key link in the process of selling. More and more companies are spending bigger amounts on the selection and the training of their salesmen. They consider this to be of prime importance. Companies which train their salesmen thoroughly find high rates of wastage of their salesmen to other companies anxious to benefit from the employment of well-trained capable salesmen.

The salesman has been described as the vital link. The part he plays in the economy of the country is certainly vital. Even though the economy may expand, unless the salesman ensures that his firm's goods are well presented and persuasively sold to buyers these goods will not reach the consumer.

In fulfilling this role the salesman acts as a spur to the economy; in selling his goods he is ensuring the employment of the workers in his firm's factory. In turn this means continued prosperity to the suppliers of materials and services to the factory and employment for the suppliers' workpeople. The tradesmen who supply the personal needs of the workpeople benefit and a chain reaction of prosperity is built up. The salesman's function, therefore, is far wider than the mere persuasion of buyers to place orders. In society he occupies an important worthwhile role and he contributes materially to the expansion of the economy.

When examined in greater detail the salesman's function covers a wide range of activities which can, dependent upon individual company policy, include some or all of the following:

1 The presentation, demonstration and sale of his company's goods. Negotiation on quality, price and delivery. Explanation and presentation of company policy.
2 The continuous examination of the market and reporting on competitive methods, products and prices. Reporting on shortages, oversupply and changes in trading conditions. The relaying to his company of any information of general commercial value.
3 The maintenance of adequate stocks of his company's goods by distributors and users. Care in ensuring that customers keep the goods under suitable storage conditions.
4 The advice and instruction of dealers and their staff in the sale and display of his company's products.
5 The continuous acquisition of knowledge of his company's products and their applications, selling points and the benefits to the user.
6 Prospecting for new outlets and new business and the extension of his company's influence on his territory.
7 The obtaining and maintenance of satisfactory displays for his company's goods.
8 The maintenance of good customer relations.

9 Recommendation of credit for customers, assessment of their premises, organization, standing and influence in the trade and the acquisition of satisfactory trade references.

10 The collection of outstanding accounts and avoidance of bad debts.

11 The handling of complaints from distributors and users.

12 Implementation of sales promotion schemes.

13 The maintenance of satisfactory records of customers' business with his company and the expeditious handling of correspondence.

14 The proper care and maintenance of any of his company's property which has been entrusted to his charge.

In carrying out his function the salesman has tools and techniques. These tools and techniques can be developed and learnt. The tools are the salesman's personality, his knowledge and judgment and his power of persuasion. The techniques are his preparation and planning, his approach to the buyer, the demonstration and presentation of his products, his methods of negotiation and finally the methods he uses to close the sale.

The Salesman's Role in Relation to Other Functions

Selling is part of the overall marketing function and, therefore, is linked to other marketing activities. It is helpful to understand the role of the salesman in relation to other functions of the enterprise and a definition of marketing is a good starting point.

The Chartered Institute of Marketing's definition is; 'Marketing is the management process responsible for identifying, anticipating and satisfying customer requirements profitably'.

Marketing practice has two main facets; the first is the information input and comprises marketing research in all its forms and the second is the promotional output. The latter includes the sales force, sales administration, advertising and sales promotion.

Selling is closely linked with the other elements of the promotional output and the link should always be both identifiable and complementary. A few examples will show how the linkage can be achieved. A company which produces and sells heavy machinery will probably publicize its technical merits and may well employ qualified mechanical engineers as salesmen. The link between the publicity appeal and the calibre and qualifications of the salesmen is obvious. Similarly, the sales administration of an enterprise should always deal with correspondence in a way which complements and supports the salesmen. The closest linkage is probably with sales promotion. In many enterprises, the salesman is responsible for carrying out the sales promotion tasks, in others there may be special sales promotion teams. Whichever system is used, it is axiomatic that the sales promotion activities must be closely co-ordinated with those of the salesman. A sales promotion campaign which is launched before the goods are available either in shops or warehouses may only succeed in selling the products of competitors.

Although selling is part of the promotional output it is also linked with other functions of the enterprise. In the consumer industries, the distribution system for fast turnover goods is often linked to the salesman's journey so that quick delivery can follow the placing of an order. Such close linkage between the salesman's journey and the delivery cycle helps to reduce the number of outlets which may become 'out of stock'. There is also a strong positive link in that co-ordinated sales journies and delivery cycles enable a buyer to reduce his investment in stock.

The salesman's function is often linked with the buying pattern of raw materials and the production cycle of his own company. It may be convenient to mount intensive sales drives to introduce seasonal products or to dispose of old stocks prior to the arrival of new products. A smooth regular production rate is the economic way of reducing production expenses but it may lead to the accumulation of heavy stocks of finished goods in advance of a seasonal demand. This occurs in the soft drinks industry where salesmen are active in late spring 'stocking-up' their customers before the summer demand.

In some enterprises, the salesman may be responsible for the collection of outstanding accounts and his competence here can have an important influence on his company's cash flow.

It can easily be understood that selling is far from an isolated part of the day-to-day operations of an enterprise but is closely associated with other functions and it can make an important contribution to the overall prosperity of the enterprise.

The Qualifications and Personal Attributes of a Salesman

The tools of a salesman were stated to be:
1 Personality
2 Knowledge
3 Judgment
4 Power of persuasion

Personality

Personality has been placed first because it is very important and there are a lot of misconceptions about the degree of importance. Very often it is said that 'X is a born salesman because he has the right sort of personality'. Remarks like this tend to outgrow their context and lead to such erroneous statements as 'you have to have the right sort of personality to be a successful salesman'.

Examined more critically it is probably nearer the truth to say that 'X is a likeable chap and people like to do things for him'. To say that a person has to have the right sort of personality to be successful as a salesman needs only a moment's examination to be disproved. Anyone who knows only a few successful salesmen will know that their personalities are completely different, in fact, no two people (with the possible exception of identical twins) have the same personality.

A particular kind of personality is not the key to success in selling and no particular kind of personality can guarantee success. Most successful salesmen are very much aware of their personality characteristics and have consciously developed them. They have extended their good qualities and have curtailed the bad ones so that they have become more acceptable personalities.

The personality characteristics which are most likely to help in building success as a salesman are:

Enthusiasm

This is probably the most important personality characteristic. Enthusiasm generates energy, whether mental or physical, and it vitalizes a sales presentation. It brings all the other personal qualities of a salesman to life. The enthusiast can triumph against adversity and take obstacles in his stride. This quality has the power to minimize difficulties and magnify benefits and it communicates easily to other people. Enthusiasm is not necessarily ostentatious and associated with physical vigour; it can be quiet and controlled and no less effective.

Integrity

Most salesmen have a genuine interest in people, are sincere and honest in their dealings with customers, and have a high standard of integrity. Sincerity leads to trust and confidence by the customer in the salesman and a salesman who is honest and sincere will gain the reputation of being a man of integrity.

Intelligence

A high intelligence is a great asset for a salesman. Unlike so many other vocations the salesman usually has to react to a customer and not only decide upon the course of action which he will follow and the method but also carry out the action immediately. The salesman does not have a chance to ask the customer to wait whilst he thinks of an answer to an objection. The quickness of the understanding of a salesman plays an important part in his ability to handle customers.

16   THE PRINCIPLES AND PRACTICE OF SELLING

Courage

There are many different ways in which courage can be displayed. The salesman needs courage to face unpleasant situations. There are few people who can fail to admire a man who, no matter how unpleasant a task may be, will face up to it and carry it through with determination and cheerfulness.

Initiative

Salesmen work alone nearly all of their working time and they work without close direction. The personal initiative and resourcefulness which they can use are considerable. Essentially a salesman must recognize opportunities and then have the initiative to seize them.

Reliability

When a promise is made it should be kept and attempts to extract promises which a salesman is doubtful of being able to keep should be resisted at all costs. There are often occasions when a buyer has a choice of suppliers and the differences in price and quality are small. On such occasions and, indeed even when the differences are great, the reliability of the salesman and his company can be the deciding factors.

Determination

The quality of determination is often associated with ruthlessness and the disregard of other people's interests. The salesman needs determination not to ride roughshod over people but to maintain his own energy in the right direction and to help him overcome difficulties.

Confidence

Confidence in one's product or service, in one's company and oneself give a conviction to anything which the salesman says. Self confidence is a solid moral prop and the absence of this quality is immediately obvious to a buyer. It is probably true to say that any salesman without self-confidence will never succeed.

Industry

The salesman, working as he does without close supervision, has many temptations to avoid. He can start late and finish early and he can spend longer with his friendly customers and less time with the awkward ones. A sense of diligence or industry is essential to a man who is trusted to do his work on his own. To be trusted creates self esteem and salesmen who are trusted should respond by being diligent, conscientious and industrious.

Self control

Experienced salesmen can always recall the many times that a situation has developed which has taxed their self control. No matter what the cause of the trouble may be and no matter how unjust the accusations, a salesman must always remain in control of himself. Loss of self control may lead to the irreparable loss of goodwill and the permanent loss of a customer. Good self control helps the salesman to accept the elations and disappointments which occur in his day-to-day work. This quality tends to bring an emotional balance and a more calm and detached judgment.

Courtesy

Courtesy in speech and manner combined with a neat and well-groomed appearance will create a favourable first impression. Courtesy is a quality which shows consideration for others and is associated with unselfishness and the absence of self interest. It is a valuable quality in creating a friendly atmosphere.

Friendliness

A warm, friendly, but not over familiar conduct creates a favourable impression. The same genuine interest in people, which characterises sincerity, is a sign of friendliness and a desire for amicable personal relations based on a regard for others.

Modesty

Modesty of claims for products and services are more impressive than exaggerated claims which later turn out to be unsubstantiated. Customers will place greater trust in salesmen who give honest, matter-of-fact opinions and are at pains to avoid using phrases containing superlatives. A modest manner on the part of the salesman is more likely to relax a buyer than an overconfident bearing which may put a buyer on the defensive.

Knowledge

A salesman needs knowledge as a tool just as much as he needs a developed personality. The knowledge which he should endeavour to acquire is wide and takes time to accumulate. It should cover the following fields.

The Salesman's own company

1 The history and development and in particular the circumstances which led to the establishment of the company.
2 The existing organization together with an organigramme showing the organizational structure and the lines of responsibility.

3 The policies, methods of implementation and the reasoning from which the policies evolved.
4 The personalities who have built up and have been associated with the company in the past and the leading figures in the current organization.

The Product or Services

1 The raw materials, their processing, characteristics and benefits to the finished product.
2 The quality standards and how they have been developed as well as their influence on performance standards.
3 The prices and terms and calculations of the percentage margins of profit which can be earned by distributors.
4 The packaging and any special features for the preservation, presentation and handling of the product.
5 The delivery arrangements and the service offered and any guarantees which may be given.
6 The current publicity programme, its nature and scope and the objectives which it is hoped to achieve.

Competition

1 Competitive policies, methods, organization and financial associations.
2 Competitive products and the standards of performance in comparison with the salesman's own products.
3 Competitive prices, terms and credit policy compared with those of the salesman's own company.
4 Competitive packaging and its design features as well as its functional value as a protection to the product.
5 Competitive delivery arrangements and service facilities in comparison with those offered by the salesman's own company.
6 Competitive publicity and its apparent objectives, the media chosen and, if possible, an estimate of the expenditure involved.

General trade information

1 Financial backing of customers or potential customers and, if possible, the share of the equity held and identity of the backers.
2 Financial associations of customers and the strength of those associations whether they be within the same trade or industry or in another.
3 Informal links of a friendly or family connection between businesses also within or outside the same trade or industry.
4 Particular specialities in merchandise stocked or services rendered by customers which merit special attention by the salesman's company.

5 Any other links between customers and manufacturers or suppliers who are competing with the salesman's company.
6 General trends or developments in the particular industries which are the salesman's concern and the possible repercussions on the existing trading pattern.

Human relations

1 An understanding of himself and his strengths and weaknesses.
2 An understanding of other peoples' motives and how to influence them.
3 An appreciation of his own personal qualities and those of other people, particularly those of his customers.
4 The ability to interpret the moods and idiosyncrasies of buyers.
5 A good general knowledge and an understanding of current events.

The territory

1 The geographical boundaries or limitations in regard to categories of customers or both.
2 The location of customers and potential customers and their areas or spheres of operation.
3 The restrictions of early closing days, special buying days and times and, where applicable, local special holidays.
4 The most direct or economical route between customers and also convenient parking places.
5 The pattern of trade, the trends and developments that are taking place and the likely repercussions on his company's trade in the territory.
6 The personal characteristics of individual customers and potential customers.

Judgment

Judgment is mainly a matter of experience and practice but an intelligent interpretation of events and the application of the interpretation to future decisions plays a major part in good judgment.

A salesman must develop judgment very early in his career if he is to be successful in his calling. The judgments which he has to exercise can cover:

1 The kind of sales arguments likely to appeal to individual buyers.
2 The methods of presenting different sales arguments.
3 The moment when it is opportune to ask for an order.

There are many other instances and every day at almost every call a salesman is called upon to exercise his judgment. Sometimes a buyer will rely very heavily on the salesman's judgment and almost place the responsibility for ordering goods on the salesman's shoulders. At other times the salesman has the task of persuading the customer that his judgment is better than the customer's.

The salesman must consciously form judgments of the buyer's moods and his main buying interests or motives.

Power of Persuasion

The prime object of the salesman's vocation is to persuade people to buy. Buyers are constantly approached by salesmen, many of them offering similar goods at similar prices and it is the salesman with the greatest power of persuasion who is likely to book the order.

Persuasion is the art of convincing people that the offer of goods or services which is made meets their individual requirements satisfactorily. For persuasion to be successful it is firstly essential to establish the true needs of the buyer and to be convinced oneself that the goods or services on offer will meet those needs satisfactorily. It is not good or clever salesmanship to sell something which will turn out to be unsatisfactory for the buyer. A salesman is in a position of trust and to maintain that position he must be a man of integrity with a responsible code of ethics.

Within the limits prescribed above, a salesman can arouse the buyer's interest and demonstrate how his needs can be met by the product or service offered. This can only be done effectively when the true needs of the buyer have been established and the benefits of the product have been demonstrated or shown to satisfy those needs.

Ways and Means of Self-development

The qualities and attributes necessary to improve standards of salesmanship can be developed by critical self-analysis and the conscious correction of faults, by watching successful people at work and learning from them and by the intelligent use of experience.

Personality

A personality can be improved in the following ways.

Enthusiasm

Enthusiasm is the outward manifestation of an alert and vigorous mind. It can be conveyed to a buyer and becomes immediately apparent to him in the animation shown by the salesman. Enthusiasm can be demonstrated by the alert, animated manner of the salesman, and by variations in the pitch and volume of his voice. An enthusiastic salesman moves and demonstrates his products with vigour, he stands erect and avoids postures which are slovenly and give the impression that he is suffering from fatigue. The quality of enthusiasm need not always be associated with physical movement and vigour. Many enthusiasts are quiet, slow-moving people who concentrate their energies and achieve results with an economy of action. Enthusiasm can be developed only by taking an active interest in something and committing oneself to the project. The enthusiast is always genuine and commits himself fully. The salesman can develop his own enthusiasm by taking a deep personal interest in his job, his company and his customers. Enthusiasm and mental and physical fitness are very closely related. The mental and physical demands on a salesman are considerable and he needs reserves of energy. He should plan his recreation with physical fitness in mind.

Integrity

This quality has to be real; it cannot be switched on and off. Fortunately most salesmen like their fellow humans and take a genuine interest in them. Integrity comes from a belief in the value of truth and honesty and a wish to perform one s task to the best of one's ability. In having such beliefs and in facing the truth, no matter how awkward and unpleasant it may be, a salesman develops strength of character, integrity and sincerity. Integrity is a very much respected quality and a salesman can develop it and enhance his reputation if he pays scrupulous regard to the honesty and truth of his claims and never knowingly misleads his customers. Customers can forgive some shortcomings in a salesman if his integrity is beyond reproach.

Intelligence

Intelligence cannot be acquired as can some of the other personal qualities which are useful to a salesman. It is really quickness of understanding or comprehension and whilst a person of limited intelligence is most unlikely to develop a high intelligence, there are ways of improving intelligence. Comprehension comes from the observation of phenomena and interpretation of the observations in a logical manner. Acute observation by a salesman can lead to a sharpening of his faculties and a realization of the value and the interpretation of these observations. The salesman should seek out the reasons behind decisions and, as his curiosity is satisfied, his intelligence will develop.

Courage

The development of courage is a formidable task and one that requires considerable willpower. It can be done by the determined tackling of jobs and problems which appear at first sight to be beyond the abilities of the individual concerned. It is true that a person cannot really know if a task is impossible until he has tried to do it. Many achievements have been recorded because of the courage and determination of individuals. The salesman who wishes to develop his courage should seek out the unpalatable problems and deliberately set himself the task of overcoming them. Very often only one success of this nature is sufficient to give enough courage to tackle any problems that arise in the future.

Initiative

Initiative, like courage, requires a conscious effort but once begun it is easy to continue. The first steps in developing initiative are for the salesman to examine his performance and his customer's buying records. From the examination he should select some weakness and should decide how to tackle and overcome it. If, for some time he has tried to sell to a customer without success he should analyse the situation and think about it until he finds a new method to try. When examining his customer's records the salesman can consider if there are any other types of customers who may have a use for his products. He will never know unless he tries to sell to them. A few successes of this nature will demonstrate the value of initiative and the salesman will quickly develop the resource to continue this activity.

Reliability

In some industries broken promises are the rule rather than the exception. It is invidious to single them out but a wise salesman always keeps a reserve when he makes a commitment to a buyer. If a promise is likely to be broken it is the salesman's responsibility to inform his buyer immediately and to give him the full facts which have caused the promise to be broken. Inevitably most firms and salesmen have, at some time or other, given promises which have been subsequently broken. Provided immediate action is taken to advise the buyers and efforts made to satisfy their needs most buyers will accept an occasional broken promise as a natural 'hazard' of commercial life. Failure to admit and to notify shortcomings immediately creates an impression of unreliability. A salesman who is straightforward in such matters demonstrates by his action that he is concerned with giving a reliable service.

Determination

A determined man is a singleminded man who, in spite of objections and handicaps, steadfastly pursues a consistent course of action. It is not an easy quality to cultivate but a salesman should develop it because it gives him an objective. Each handicap is a challenge which with determination can probably be overcome. The easiest way to become determined is to respond to challenges or to seek them out and tackle them with vigour and to keep at them until they have been overcome.

Confidence

Lack of confidence communicates itself to a buyer immediately. A salesman should build his confidence before he sees his buyer. To do this he should equip himself with knowledge of his product or service, the market, the buyer, and he should also have a conviction in the value of his product. Confidence grows from conviction and the salesman who studies his job seriously quickly gains confidence. It is important to avoid nervous mannerisms which may distract buyers and show lack of composure and lack of confidence.

Industry

Diligence or industry is largely a matter of self pride. There is much truth in the old saying that 'if a job's worth doing, it's worth doing well'. Doing a job to the best of one's ability gives a sense of satisfaction and a sense of achievement. The salesman needs only a sense of justice to be industrious. He is trusted to work without close supervision and, in most people, the conscience is the hardest taskmaster. The industrious salesman makes his first call as early as possible and his last call at the latest possible time. He also plans his sales presentation to make the most effective use of his time whilst he is with the buyer.

Self control

'Count ten before you answer' is one way of developing self-control, but buyers may notice a fixed expression and silently moving lips. Habitual self-control stems from tolerance and a realization that there are usually two sides to an argument. The salesman should always try to see the other side because not only does he develop self-control, he also becomes more skilled in overcoming problems if he understands them. The cultivation of tolerance and understanding and a patient attitude will develop the salesman's self-control.

Courtesy

True courtesy springs from consideration of the needs of others. Flowery speech and ostentatious manners do not show true courtesy. Those actions which are mindful of others and consider other people's feelings are courteous. Courtesy can be cultivated by a realization that attention to the needs and problems of others is a natural consideration for their comfort and well-being. It is elementary courtesy for a salesman to be neat, well-groomed and of fresh appearance; to be otherwise is to affront the status of the buyer. Such consideration usually evokes a friendly and sympathetic response.

Friendliness

A warm, friendly personality can be developed by the conscious thought that everybody has some good in them. Seek out the good points of the people who are met each day and it will be found that they will respond to the interest taken in them with the same warmth and friendliness.

Modesty

A modest manner should be cultivated by omitting superlative claims and extreme language from conversations. Exaggerations and challenging statements tend to arouse hostility in the listener. Modest phrasing and true and accurate statements which can be substantiated by facts are more convincing. Exaggerated understatements and false modesty should be avoided.

The qualities mentioned above need to be balanced so that the salesman presents himself as an acceptable personality. Some of the qualities are more important than others but it is wrong to develop any one to the exclusion of others. The salesman should try to develop them all but should be wary of any one quality becoming disproportionately important.

Knowledge

Knowledge is often acquired as the result of curiosity and it is often said that a curious mind is an intelligent mind.

The salesman with an enquiring mind can find a vast field of knowledge waiting to be explored. It should be remembered that the acquisition of knowledge for its own sake is a very barren pursuit and knowledge is of value only when it is used.

The Salesman's own company

A salesman taking an active interest in his own company should ask, if he has not already been told, the following questions:

1 When was the company founded and by whom?
2 What has been the company's trading history and development?
3 Has the company invented or introduced anything new to the market?
4 What is the general policy of the company and its marketing policy?
5 How is the company organized to carry out these policies and who are the responsible executives?
6 Has the company any associations with other companies, other markets and other countries?

The Product or Services

More detailed attention is given to the product in the next chapter.

Competition

Competition was mentioned as one of the fields where a salesman should have knowledge but, since there are wider aspects to a study of competitive activity, this has also been included in the next chapter.

General trade information

The knowledge of general trade information which a salesman can gain is quite substantial and many companies rely upon their salesmen entirely for some kinds of trade information. Sources which a salesman can explore are:

1 General information in the popular press, the trade and technical papers.
2 Published reports by government departments, industrial working parties, royal or special commissions, trade association and research bodies. Some interesting reports have also been published by professional institutes and technical associations.
3 Contact with and conversations with his customers about general trade matters.
4 Published statistics by government departments, industrial and trade associations.
5 His own company management and the service departments such as market research, advertising, product research and development departments.

Human relations

Acquiring a knowledge of human relations is largely a matter of personal observation and continuous contact with people. Salesmen are rarely qualified psychologists but the good salesman is like a psychologist in that he is continually observing the reactions of the human mind.

Before a salesman can really begin to influence others he needs to understand himself. He needs to know what other people think of him. Do they, for example, regard him with respect and admiration or do they scarcely notice him? The impression which a salesman makes depends upon many things but he should always observe very carefully the reactions of others to his own speech and actions.

It is helpful for the salesman to hear his own voice on tape; most people find this experience an unwelcome shock. By listening to a tape recording of his speech the salesman can learn to eliminate undesirable qualities. The voice should be clear and pleasant and should vary in pitch and volume. A regional accent is not a handicap but a salesman who tries to overcome one by using what he thinks is a socially superior accent usually gets the worst of both.

The salesman should always make a mental note when he is with his customers of the following kind of information.

1 The reactions of his customers to different kinds of sales arguments.
2 The personal habits of his customers.
3 The thought processes of his customers.
4 The personal and commercial interests of his customers.

In making a study of his individual buyers the salesman builds up a store of knowledge of human beings and their reactions and he learns how to handle the many different situations which can arise between buyer and seller.

As he presents his arguments in different ways to different buyers the salesman increases his knowledge of human relations and can, therefore, consciously develop himself.

The Territory

When getting to know his territory, the salesman should use a map. He will, very probably, have been provided with a map by his sales manager and his territory boundaries will, most likely, be clearly marked. If, as sometimes happens, no map has been supplied the salesman should get one because the thorough and systematic coverage of a territory can only be done with the aid of a map that has clearly defined boundaries for the salesman's territory. Where the territory is densely populated a street map will be necessary, probably, in addition to a smaller scale map which may be all that is required to show the complete territory. To know his territory thoroughly the salesman should:

1 Mark his territory boundary clearly on a map which, if possible, is of sufficiently small scale to be on one sheet of paper.
2 Mark up his customers' locations on a map, if necessary of larger scale than in 1 above, so that the whereabouts of the customers in any particular areas will be noticed.
3 Go through the classified telephone directories of the area and check that contact is being made with all possible customers.
4 Examine any trade or industrial directories at the local reference libraries.
5 Note early closing days or buyers' special buying times.
6 Keep records of his customers' buying history, preferably on cards.
7 Prepare a journey route.
8 Discuss with progressive customers the past, current and likely future trends of trade and variations in the pattern of trade.
9 Study the individual characteristics of customers and potential customers.

Judgment

It was mentioned earlier that judgment is mainly experience plus the intelligent interpretation of events.

Good judgment can be developed only by practice. Fortunately a salesman has unlimited opportunities for practising the exercise of judgment. Developing good judgment follows closely upon the study of human relations. By observing the characteristics of individual buyers and framing the sales presentation to meet these characteristics a salesman develops his judgment. As objections are raised so does a salesman learn how to exercise judgment in handling them. Similarly, as buyers react differently to different situations a salesman must learn how to cope with individual characteristics. It is from the regular practice of judgment in such cases that a salesman develops this faculty.

Power of Persuasion

One of the best ways of developing the power of persuasion is to join a debating society and to take an active part. It is good experience to propose or oppose a motion and to hear the arguments subjected to the cut and thrust of other opinions. In debating, as in selling, the debater must learn to evaluate his arguments and to gauge their effect on his listeners. The salesman, when confronted by a buyer, has a listener who is not inhibited by any debating rules from interrupting. The salesman should, whenever possible, set his sales presentation at a conversational level and by question and personal interest bring his buyer into the conversation.

In getting the buyer to take part in the conversation and in ascertaining his true needs the salesman brings the buyer into the presentation. If the buyer can be interested sufficiently to take part in a demonstration the alert salesman immediately realizes that the buyer is experiencing the satisfaction of his needs. This is one very good reason why the capable salesman always demonstrates his products.

The Salesman's Key Characteristics

Among the many personal attributes of a salesman, there are some 'key' characteristics which make the most important contributions to success in selling. They are Enthusiasm, Integrity, Intelligence, Initiative and Friendliness. When these qualities exist strongly, the salesman is able to lead and to influence others.

The development of the 'key' characteristics and their application, using the salesman's knowledge of human relations and the regular exercise of his judgement, is likely to create a well-rounded, acceptable personality which people will acknowledge and respect.

The next chapter about the product exposes some of the channels and means which may be used by the salesman to apply his personal qualities to influence buyers.

2 The Product

The salesman should obviously have a thorough knowledge of his product but it is not always realized that there are many associated fields where a thorough knowledge is equally important. The questions which customers may ask can range, as any experienced salesman will confirm, over a wide list of subjects. These subjects are usually related in some way to the product or service and it is a matter of importance that the salesman should be able to give a convincing answer.

The associated fields which a salesman should explore, so that he can provide answers, include packaging, competitive products, the service which his company may offer and the advertising claims of his own company and those of his competitors.

The knowledge which a salesman gains of his product and the associated fields gives him an authority with his customers and earns for him their respect.

Some salesmen and sales managers assert that competitive products and activities should be ignored and that all the energies of the sales personnel should be devoted to the selling of their own products. This assertion is an attractive one but can very rarely be followed because many customers insist on product comparisons. The salesman who has not taken the trouble to compare his own products with those of his competitors and to isolate the advantages will often miss opportunities of pressing home decisive selling points.

The acquisition of product knowledge should not be left to chance or picked up as the salesman goes about his job. Information learnt in this way is usually incomplete and ill-balanced so that the learner gains distorted knowledge. A salesman who has gathered his product knowledge in this way is often, unwittingly, guilty of misconceptions which he passes on to his customers. Customers are often as knowledgeable as the salesman and quickly realize that the salesman who has incomplete or inaccurate product knowledge is unlikely to be able to give them the advice or service which they require.

The salesman who wishes to build a store of product knowledge should set about the task in a systematic way. He should set down the kind of knowledge that he thinks will be useful and should methodically go through the likely sources until he is satisfied that the information he is acquiring is both authoritative and complete for his needs. A cautionary note is necessary in that a salesman, particularly in a semi-technical field, may be tempted to acquire just enough knowledge to delude himself into believing that he is an expert. This may cause him to refrain from asking for the help of specialist technicians who are maintained by his company for the benefit of customers.

The kind of knowledge which a salesman needs will obviously vary with the product or service which he sells, and the type of customer with whom he conducts business. The easiest way to acquire knowledge of the product is to start at the beginning with the basic ingredients or the raw materials.

Examination of the Raw Materials and Processes Used

With many products the examination of the raw materials can be a fascinating study. Man's ingenuity in taking natural products and using their special properties for his own needs has been one of the methods by which civilization has developed. Even a casual reading of history reveals the association of the discovery and use of natural resources with the rise and fall of different countries.

The kind of enquiries which the salesman should make about the product and its origin are:

What are the raw materials from which the product is made?

Many products are made of a combination of different raw materials and the salesman should try to isolate them.

Where do the raw materials come from?

The origin of the raw materials may have a special significance to some buyers. They may have served overseas in the forces in the country of origin and, therefore, have more than a passing interest in the raw material. In the cases where the world's supply of a raw material comes from one source this knowledge is necessary and pertinent if an unsettled political or economic situation arises.

What are the basic qualities of the raw materials?

Many raw materials are used because of the special properties which they possess and which make them particularly suitable for doing certain kinds of work. A salesman would be failing in the elementary duty of keeping his buyers accurately informed if he had not made himself aware of the basic qualities of the raw materials. Examples which spring to mind are chamois leather, sea island cotton and the whole new ranges of plastic products. An examination of the basic qualities and how these qualities give the raw material and ultimately the product the special properties which enable it to do certain kinds of work better than any other material is an important piece of knowledge. When a product has a raw material which comes into this category the salesman can use such knowledge most effectively.

Have the raw materials any historical associations?

This information may be of general interest only but biblical or historical associations may often arrest the wandering attention of a buyer. A sales presentation often needs a lighter side during which the buyer and seller can relax for a few moments on a topic of interest and relevance but not necessarily of first importance. Snippets of information which can be associated with historical events can often provide the means to produce a relaxed atmosphere.

How are the raw materials created?

Too often the origin of the raw materials are taken for granted and, particularly in some of the retail trades, this can lead to mis-statements. The raw materials may be mined or grown, they may come from shrubs or trees or from animals. They may be chemical products or a mixture of several things and the salesman who is aware of the origin of the raw materials in his product demonstrates the range of his knowledge.

Who discovered the raw materials and who accumulates them?

Again this information may be of passing interest but every schoolboy knows that Sir Walter Raleigh brought tobacco to Britain. The story of pearl divers and how they get the pearls is an interesting one. Items of information which have an arresting quality and which hold the attention of buyers are a necessary part of the good salesman's stock in trade.

How do the raw materials reach the factory?

This may be a simple matter of transportation in an open railway truck but there may be an interesting story which can be told. The transport of logs, held together by a hawser and towed by a tug is a fascinating sight and other raw materials may have similarly unusual methods of transportation.

Many of the questions which have been posed can be answered by the management of the salesman's own company. Sometimes management, assured in the possession of knowledge, takes for granted that the same knowledge is possessed by the salesman. If management does not inform the salesman he should set out his questions and ask them methodically when the opportunity arises. Another good source of information is the public reference library which is available in most districts. The librarians can be very helpful in suggesting sources of information. There may be trade or professional associations with local branches in the salesman's district and the secretaries will often be pleased to suggest sources of information or even the names of individuals who are authorities on particular subjects.

When the salesman has satisfied himself that his knowledge of the raw materials is sufficient for his needs he should commence his enquiries into the processing.

The questions he should ask are:

Are the raw materials treated in any way such as ageing, fortifying, drying, soaking, blending and refining?

The salesman should find out what happens to the product and what the process is so that he can talk intelligently about it to his customers.

How are such processes carried out and what is the reason for them?

Having discovered what the processing consists of, the salesman should find out how it works and why it has been used. For example, does the process strengthen the product, improve its appearance, or make it more satisfactory in some other respect?

How is the product manufactured?

The raw materials may be processed in order to prepare them for manufacture as leather is tanned or copper refined and made into billets or ingots and then rolled or drawn into plates and rods. During the manufacturing process blending may take place as happens to whisky where different kinds of whisky are blended to give a balanced blend suitable for most palates. The manufacture may be to a set design and the salesmen should know how this is done.

Why is the product treated or designed in such a manner?

Blending, for example, is often a matter of taste which has been developed through years of experience. Scotch whisky distillers know that a strong whisky which is light in colour is more acceptable in the United States of America and they blend accordingly. The salesman who takes the trouble to find this type of information shows that his company considers its markets intelligently. The reasons for certain designs being used during the manufacture may reveal advantageous selling points. The designs may be to improve the strength or adaptability of the product or improve the appearance.

What quality control tests are applied during manufacture? What is the nature of these tests and how have the standards been set?

The background of information about tests and standards is essential to a salesman when the buyer demands details of specifications and performance data. There is a big difference between 60 m.p.h. downhill with a following wind and the average of a measured mile covered in both directions on a flat stretch of ground with no wind. The conditions under which different firms will use the salesman's product may vary immensely and the salesman must be prepared to answer all kinds of questions about the performance of his product.

Have there been any changes in the development of the product since it was first introduced? What were the changes and why were they made?

The history of the development of the product may be revealed and the successful research which has led to improvements. The salesman may be able to point with pride to the progressive and enterprising character of his company and its ability to incorporate technological improvements.

Who invented or developed the product? Is the product exclusive and covered by patents?

There are many companies which have developed products that achieved world renown in their field because of discoveries made by them. Even if the particular product is no longer in use and has been replaced by a later invention or development the salesman can take pride in knowing that, at one time, his company led the field. Knowledge of patent protection is of value in case the salesman comes across imitators. In such instances he should report them immediately to his Head Office.

Is the product manufactured under any special conditions such as sterility, pressure or heat and do these conditions have any special significance?

Although this question belongs properly to the method of manufacture there can be special reasons such as the use of stainless steel vessels in the food manufacturing industry. This is because most of the other metals contain some lead and oxidize more easily. The regulations covering the lead content in food are particularly strict because lead is a cumulative poison.

Are there any special skills in manufacturing the product?

If craftsmen are employed and special skills are needed it is very helpful if the salesman is fully cognizant of them. When talking about the quality of his product a brief description of the kind of craftsmen who are employed and the skills necessary to produce a high quality article can be very convincing to a buyer who is comparing products and is unaware of some of the finer points of quality.

How is the product packaged? Is any special kind of package used to protect or preserve the product?

Many improvements have been made in recent years in packaging techniques. The quality and design have changed considerably and the introduction of flexible packaging made of plastic films has improved the presentation of many products. There may be particular technical aspects of packaging such as waterproofing, heat resisting and protection from rough handling which are valid sales points. The design aspect of the package may be of particular importance for goods which are displayed in supermarkets and chain stores and are often bought on impulse.

How is the product advertised?

Advertising is often a provocative subject on which many opinions are aired. The salesman should try to avoid controversy and should do his best to be informative. The background of his approach to advertising should be his knowledge of the company policy. It is helpful if the salesman has been supplied with a statement of the company's advertising aims, the methods followed and the desired results. The salesman should know in detail what methods have been used and should have a schedule showing the television times and dates, the newspapers to be used and insertion dates and should have 'pulls' or specimen copies of the advertisements which will appear. In the case of television advertisements a story board should be provided which can be shown to customers. The reasons for using the type of art work and copy and for making a particular kind of appeal should be known by the salesman. A full knowledge of the company advertising plans helps the salesman to explain to his customers, if they are in the distributive trades, what his company is doing for them.

Some of the questions about the processes may be considered to infringe on trade secrets by the management of the company and it may not be possible for the salesman to acquire all the information which he would like. The frank questioning of management on processes is the best way to gain the knowledge as this is the only really reliable source. Most companies are prepared to disseminate information to their salesmen and are favourably impressed by those who have taken the trouble to seek out knowledge and who try to improve their selling efficiency.

Investigation into User Requirements and the Suitability of the Product for these Requirements

To do his job properly the salesman needs to know, not only as much as possible about his product, but what the basic needs of the user are and how close the product comes to meeting those needs. In some cases this may present difficulties because the salesman's customers may be distributors who have the sole rights to supply users. Attempts by the salesman to get in touch with users may be regarded by distributors with the suspicion that the salesman or his company want to cut out the distributor and supply the users direct. There are also difficulties when the user is the housewife and she buys from a retail shop. The salesman does not have the time to seek out housewives and subject them to a cross examination. In such cases the salesman's company may employ a market research organization.

Whenever it is possible for the salesman to get to know users and to do so without sacrificing too much of his time or antagonizing distributors he should make the attempt. The knowledge which a salesman can gain from direct contact with the user and by seeing his product in use is invaluable. Until a salesman has experienced user contact his knowledge is theoretical and tends to lack the conviction of practical experience. Contact with users is not so important for all types of products but is essential for the salesmen of, say, office equipment and for most goods which involve capital expenditure.

The information which a salesman needs to know can be found from the answers to the following questions:

Who uses the product?

This is obviously the basic question which the salesman should ask and his investigation should then be developed.

Is the user a craftsman or craftswoman with special skills?

The salesman needs to know the specialist skills which may be needed particularly if he is asked by a potential customer about the methods of use and the kind of labour required. The salesman may also be asked questions about the training of operatives. Unless the salesman can answer questions of this nature accurately he may lose the sale or perhaps install equipment which will be used ineffectively and lead to complaints.

How is the product used and what is the method of use?

This part of the salesman's enquiry is most important and the salesman should observe the operation carefully. If it is possible for the salesman to do the operation himself he should attempt it so that he will be familiar with the process and may experience some of the snags which arise. The practical experience gained will be of value whenever operating difficulties arise in the future.

Is the product used in association with any other products and how is it affected by them?

Unless the salesman is aware of circumstances such as these he may often be dealing with complaints which are not attributable to his product at all. Some manufacturers take the precaution of restricting gurantees on their products unless the materials used in conjunction with them are on a 'recommended' list. Where different materials can be used there is always the opportunity when complaints arise for one supplier to put the blame on to another supplier's material. A salesman who has not investigated this aspect of the use of his product puts himself into a vulnerable position.

Are any tools or instruments used with the product and are there any significant reasons for the particular tools or instruments?

Many manufacturers of equipment supply special tools which are designed for the use of mechanics and service personnel. Failure to use these tools can result in damage to the equipment and loss of performance. Many mechanics and service men have received a general training which is insufficient to cope with the specialist machines, made by individual manufacturers. Ignorance on maintenance and repair problems can lead to complaints and, on occasions, expensive breakdowns.

What kind of performance does the user expect from the product?

Standards of performance are often decisive factors in making the sale. The standards may refer to tolerances, quality as per sample, performances in speed or output and any of the wide demands which buyers sometimes make. The salesman should find precisely what the buyer expects from the product as he cannot hope to give satisfaction without establishing the real needs.

What are the keeping qualities of the product or normal life with fair wear and tear?

The salesman should have acquired this information from the experience of his own company over the years. The depreciation of stock is a matter of importance to both traders and users and the salesman should be able to answer any questions decisively and accurately.

What are the advantages and disadvantages of the product to the user?

The collection of knowledge of the pros and cons of the product during use should be a continuous activity of the salesman. From this information he can build a series of practical selling points and can forestall objections. The information should also be fed back to the salesman's Head Office so that advantage may be taken to consider possible modifications in the future.

Does the user have any particular problems with the product and, if so, what are they?

Major problems, almost always, will be referred back to the salesman so that he is given the opportunity of correcting the situation. The salesman should not presume that this will happen inevitably and should try to keep in close touch with users so that he becomes aware of problems as soon as possible. Failure to maintain close contact can result in the loss of business and the discovery of the reason when it is too late to take corrective action. Minor problems are sometimes accepted by customers with a sense of resignation but may develop into significant ones when a competing product is offered which appears not to have the same faults. Close contact by the salesman is the only way to avoid embarrassing situations of this nature.

Are there any improvements in the product which the user would like?

A salesman should be cautious when following this enquiry as too much enthusiasm in this direction may bring demands which the salesman's company cannot possibly meet. The salesman should always take a responsible view of his company's interests. Major alterations to product specifications are expensive and, unless they are likely to gain a worthwhile share of the market, will probably be unprofitable.

Does the product have any residual or ancillary use apart from its main use?

The extension of the use of the product for some other purpose has often been used as a major selling point. In the food industry it is common to pack products in a container which has a continued use after the contents have been expended. Many raw materials have a recovery value particularly in chemical processing where solutions, after use, may be passed through a recovery plant and re-used.

Is the product packaged in the most convenient form for the user?

Many people have had the experience of buying some product which was badly packaged. Some packages are difficult to open and once opened cannot be adequately re-closed. some packages burst or will not stack, others spill when the contents are poured. The salesman should note carefully how the product is used and where the container is placed in relation to the operation. Does the container facilitate or restrict the use of the product? Does the container look pleasing and does it enhance the product?

Is the product supplied in a satisfactory manner?

Sometimes products are mishandled in transit because the wrong method of carriage is used. Breakages and spoilage may occur and cause dissatisfaction. If the salesman has the opportunity of seeing the goods arrive at his customer's premises he can see for himself. Any suggestions for improvements should, of course, be advised to his Head Office.

Is the after sales service satisfactory?

There are many products which need after-sales services for a short period after the initial purchase. There are others which may require this service throughout their normal life. The availability and the quality of the service offered should be such that the user has confidence in both the product and the after-sales service.

The investigation into user requirements may be a time consuming occupation but once completed it gives the salesman very valuable background for handling customers and provided the knowledge gained is kept up to date it will stand him in good stead throughout his selling career.

The difficulties of user contact should not be minimized when distributors are involved and the salesman has much to gain by being frank and forthright. If access to the user of the goods is through a distributor the salesman would be well advised to ask the distributor to introduce him and if necessary send a member of his staff with him on a visit to a user. Some distributors will realize the benefits which they will gain from having a capable, well-informed manufacturer's representative working in co-operation with them.

The Analysis of Competitive Products, Prices, Policies and Methods

The physical analysis or technical examination of a competitor's products is properly a matter for the research, technical or development departments of the salesman's company.

In some instances a laboratory examination may be necessary before a worthwhile analytical comparison can be made and this is obviously quite beyond the resources of a salesman. Companies which are faced with problems of almost scientific analysis often have a research section which specializes in this kind of work. Too often, unfortunately, the reports which are produced are so technical that most salesmen would have difficulty in understanding them and too often the information is not passed on to salesmen.

Even though the technical comparison may be beyond the salesman's resources he should ask his own management for information of comparative analyses between his own and competitive products. Some managements refuse to divulge this kind of information on the grounds that it is no concern of the salesman. This is a rather shortsighted policy because customers often insist on product comparisons and openly challenge salesmen to match the performance of competing goods.

Some companies publish comparative product data to their salesmen and, of course, draw attention to the particular points of superiority of their own products.

The salesman should consider competitive products in a systematic way and should follow the same sort of analytical approach which was suggested as a means of acquiring information about his own products.

The kind of information which he should try to obtain is:

A comparative analysis of the fundamental qualities of competitive products and his own.

This should cover such points as the material used and its quality.

A comparative analysis of design features and assessment of the functional value when the product is in use.

A comparison of design features which are decorative and enhance the appearance is a difficult task. Most people can see the difference between an old-fashioned design and a modern design but when the cycle of fashion turns completely the old suddenly becomes new again. Comparisons which are a matter of taste are probably best made by salesmen because their judgment tends to be influenced by the degree of consumer acceptability of the design. This is probably as effective a form of judgment as any and after all, consumer acceptability will decide the success or failure of the design.

A comparative analysis of weight or volume for price or performance, if it can be measured in absolute terms.

This may be one of the popular comparisons made by buyers because it is simple and reduces products to a common factor.

A comparative analysis of the packages or containers.

These should be examined for protection of the product, ease of handling and use, ease of stacking and storage, ease of identification of contents and ease of opening and closing. The attractiveness of the packages should be compared. Packaging can be very important and often, when a choice is available, the most acceptable package will decide the issue if the differences in price and quality are small. It is also worth examining the packages to see if there is any possible after use advantage.

A comparison of the publicized selling features and advertising claims of competitors' products with his own.

These are the points to which a buyer's attention is constantly directed. Most companies try to select a unique selling point on which advertising claims can be made without fear of contradiction. The salesman should examine these claims carefully because, on occasions, although the selling point may be undeniably unique it has no merit and does not benefit the buyer.

A comparison of prices, trade margins, discounts and credit policies.

In some trades this is an easy task because there may be only a few manufacturers, all of whom are selling well known products at publicized prices. In other trades it can be very difficult because of varied methods of distribution, differences between products, acute competition and a host of other reasons. A salesman should, nevertheless, try to obtain as much information about competitive prices as he can. There are always some buyers who will stoutly maintain that they can buy the same article elsewhere but at a lower price. The salesman who has studied competitive prices can assess the accuracy of such a claim and decide how to deal with it effectively.

The salesman should examine the selling policies, the methods and organizations of his competitors.

Apart from learning of the extent of the competition which he has to combat the salesman may find methods which he can use to build his own turnover.

An examination of the publicity and sales promotion methods of competitors.
This may reveal new and unexploited sources of business which the salesman can follow up.

Finally, in looking at competitive activity the salesman should study the selling techniques of his competitors.

If he can discover their most popular sales arguments and claims, he can develop a sales presentation which will combat those of his competitors. The acquisition of knowledge of competitor's selling tactics can influence the tactics of the salesman and may, on some occasions, forewarn him of future competitive policy developments.

It is not sufficient for the salesman to make comparisons of competitive activity. After all, the buyer will judge all comparisons from his own viewpoint and, therefore, the salesman should try to establish the buyer's main interests as soon as possible. Having established them, the salesman can make comparisons of sales features between products in relation to the buyer's main interests. A phrase such as 'As you are primarily interested in performance, you will be pleased to know that our machine has an output of X per hour which is higher than any other machine on the market', demonstrates the relation of a comparison to a buyer's main interest.

The main buying interests are listed below with a brief explanation of each.

Performance

This may be the production rate per minute, it may be the rate of stock turn of a fast-selling consumer good or it may be the wearing qualities of a driving belt. Each kind of product has its own performance standards.

Economy

For most products, economy means the durability in relation to the price or the running costs in relation to output and capital expenditure.

The kind of economic yardstick may vary from one buyer to another.

Durability

This main buying interest is usually considered in relation to economy. But there can be notable exceptions in the case, for instance, of machinery.

A machine may have been 'written off' and the cost recovered in depreciation but the machine continues to function.

The author has seen a one hundred year old British textile spinning 'machine' still in regular use in a developing country.

Appearance

It may be difficult to make an objective comparison of appearance as aesthetic judgements are often a matter of taste. One needs to take account of contemporary majority opinion.

Safety

This interest is usually a tangible one such as fail-safe switches, machine guards, non-flammable textiles and the guarantee of hygienically prepared or sterilized foods.

Comfort

Usually this interest is personal and applies to clothes, beds, chairs, and other goods of a similar personal nature. It can, however, be an abstract interest of having say, the comfort of a sound insurance policy.

Adaptability

The versatility in use of a product is its adaptability. Multi-use products have increased considerably during the present technological age. But versatility may be at the expense of performance.

Publicity Support

This is usually a supporting interest although some buyers are attracted by particular appeals and assume that the attraction is universal.

Distribution and Service

The delivery service, local availability of stock and service facilities can be a major interest. The availability and quality of an after-sales service may be a decisive factor in making the sale.

All claims made on behalf of products can be placed under one or other of these main buying interests. Quite often one claim may come under more than one heading as in the case of an electric drill with attachments. One might claim that its versatility gives Performance, Economy and Adaptability.

The salesman should note all the claims that he can find for his own product and then classify them under the nine headings and put the same claim under more than one heading if it is appropriate. After classification it will be helpful if he considers each claim in comparison with competitors' products and then grades his own claims as advantages over their products and, therefore, major selling points; or as benefits which are equal to those of his competitors or as disadvantages.

By making such an examination the salesman can produce a table like that shown in Table 2.1.

Table 2.1

		Advantages or Major Selling Points	Benefits equal to Competitors	Disadvantages
Performance	Own product			
	Competitor A			
	Competitor B			
Economy	Own product			
	Competitor A			
	Competitor B			
Durability	Own product			
	Competitor A			
	Competitor B			
Appearance	Own product			
	Competitor A			
	Competitor B			
Safety	Own product			
	Competitor A			
	Competitor B			
Comfort	Own product			
	Competitor A			
	Competitor B			
Adaptability	Own product			
	Competitor A			
	Competitor B			
Publicity support	Own product			
	Competitor A			
	Competitor B			
Distribution and Service	Own product			
	Competitor A			
	Competitor B			

In such a table the salesman can prepare for himself a list of the major selling points for each main buying interest and can see at a glance how his product compares with those of his competitors. This system has the advantage of encouraging the salesman to make a critical analysis of his own and competitive products and it enables him, once the table has been compiled, to present his case with confidence.

It is obviously of importance that the salesman should make his analysis as fairly and accurately as possible and that he should recognize which main buying interest is dominant in the buyer's mind before he presents his sales arguments. There are often times when a salesman has to present his arguments quickly and by using this system he is prepared with the main selling points of his product for a concentrated presentation.

When a buyer wishes to concentrate upon one or two particular main interests the salesman is able, not only to give the advantages, but the general benefits and is prepared if necessary to discuss the disadvantages. This subject is dealt with more fully in Chapter 4.

Investigation into the Distributive Requirements

The examination of the methods by which goods are distributed has become an important subject during recent years. There have been considerable changes in the distributive trades, some of which are partly the result of legislation. Since World War II there has been a series of Acts of Parliament which has changed trading conditions:

> Monopolies and Restrictive Practices Act (1948), Restrictive Trade Practices Act (1956), Resale Price Act (1964), Misrepresentation Act (1967), Trade Descriptions Act (1968), Hire Purchase Act (1969), Unsolicited Goods and Services Act (1971-5), Trade Descriptions Act (1972), Fair Trading Act (1973), Supply of Goods (Implied Terms) Act (1973), Prices Act (1974, 1975), Unfair Contract Terms Act (1977), Consumer Safety Act (1978), Sale of Goods Act (1979).

The general effect of successive legislation has been to introduce greater competition, particularly between distributors, by the abolition of collective resale price maintenance. Another important effect has been the introduction of more stringent controls over publicity and advertising claims.

Changes have also taken place through new developments such as the necessity to install frozen food cabinets to handle frozen foods, others because of the need to meet special situations such as the growth of Do-It-Yourself activites and the shops which specialize in supplies of this nature. The rapid expansion of supermarkets carrying a wide range of merchandise is another instance and the establishment of discount houses is yet a further case.

Undoubtedly the period of change will continue and the salesman needs to be particularly alert in noticing changes and in taking advantage of them. In a period of change a difficult situation can often arise and a salesman may be faced with the dilemma of ceasing to supply an old customer and commencing to supply a new one. The situation may be aggravated by close traditional ties between a distributive trade association and the manufacturer. Since changes rarely proceed at an even pace it is not an easy decision to make and by acting too soon the old business may be lost before new business is gained. By acting too late the business may not be gained and the old business may be lost.

Sometimes new distributive channels can be opened gradually without undue embarrassment but major changes usually bring their problems.

When examining the distributive arrangements the salesman should remember his contact with the user and the question, 'Is the product supplied in a satisfactory manner?' The issues raised in the widest sense by this question should form the basis of the salesman's enquiries. He should set out to establish what kind of distribution service the user needs from his supplier.

The kind of questions which will help the salesman to find the information about the user's needs and whether he is getting a satisfactory distribution service are:

How frequently does the user buy the product?

This is an important question which will help to decide the stocks of the product which are necessary and the location of supply points. The keeping qualities of the product or its susceptibility to fashion changes will influence the decisions on the kind of distributive chain which is required.

How many users are there and where are they located?

If the potential users are the 16,000,000 households in Great Britain then obviously the product must have a considerable number of outlets. If on the other hand the product is supplied to specialist manufacturers in a small industry which is concentrated in one area the number of outlets would be few; they might even be supplied direct from the salesman's factory.

Does the user want or need to have a stock of the product?

If the product is perishable, stocks should be kept to a minimum. Most distributors and users like to keep stock as low as possible but most manufacturers prefer to dispose of finished goods to the trade as soon as possible. Limitations imposed on stock levels by the character of the product (factors such as keeping qualities, cost, fashion influence, and general availability of the product) need to be taken into account.

How big a stock should the user carry dependent upon his size of operation?

This question involves the close co-operation of both users and distributors. Apart from considerations of capital invested the full utilization of machinery or labour may be involved. In the case of distributors the dangers of being caught without stock should be assessed.

Does the user have deliveries in greater frequency from other distributors?

It is possible that the goods could be supplied more satisfactorily by a distributor in another trade. This is a point which should be examined with particular care and any soundings which the salesman may make should be done initially without commitment because of the possible repercussions from existing distributors.

Does the product require any special storage, handling or service requirements, including after sales service under guarantee?

The need for special arrangements of this nature may seriously limit the choice of distributors and perhaps involve the salesman's company in training the distributor's personnel. Care must be taken in locating distributors who give service within reasonable distance of the users who are expected to take advantage of the service.

Is any regular maintenance required on the product which should be performed by a qualified technician?

If the product requires this kind of service and it is provided by the distributor he will probably have to be an accredited agent with the franchise for a given area. Such a distributor will need to be chosen with care.

Can the user be supplied more conveniently by any other method and, if so, what is the other method?

Several examples where this has happened have occurred during the last few years. The growth in direct selling of domestic appliances and the establishment of tyre shops which give a specialist fitting service are two examples.

Are the present distributors adequate for servicing the market?

In a growing market this situation can be a problem particularly if the distributor has an area franchise.

The salesman should watch for signs such as the urgent demands for stock and the failure to supply less popular lines in a range. Evidence of failure to give an adequate delivery service often comes direct from users to manufacturers. In such cases the distributive chain should be expanded by the appointment of additional suppliers.

What distributive channels do competitors use?

As a rule most manufacturers use the same distributive channels. The exceptions are such activities as direct selling and sales through manufacturer owned retail shops. The salesman should, nevertheless, check how his competitors goods are supplied just in case they have an advantage which his own company has missed.

Are there any products with similar characteristics which are distributed through different channels?

This sometimes happens and shortly after the Second World War when supplies were difficult to obtain, most distributors tried to obtain goods outside their normal range so that their general turnover could be raised. Times of shortage are not the only stimuli to encouraging distributors to extend the range of goods handled. Competition is an equally sharp spur. Patent medicines are now widely stocked by supermarkets; ladies' hosiery is sometimes sold in the record department of music shops.

The salesman who consciously and methodically examines the channels of distribution and is alert in spotting changes may discover new and worthwhile outlets which can increase his company's share of the total trade.

Main Product Points

The salesman who masters knowledge of his product from the raw materials, through the processing, packaging, publicity to the user requirements will have a formidable background knowledge. If his knowledge also includes the competition and the distributive requirements he should be able to deal with most queries on the spot.

It is, however, always useful for the salesman to have the salient features of the product at the forefront of his mind when conversing with his customers. The salient features are the benefits which appeal to customers and how the product or service will meet his individual needs.

To apply product knowledge effectively, the salesman must always ascertain his buyers' needs and this is an important part of prospection and, later on, the sales interview.

3 Planning a Sales Journey and Prospection

The planning of a sales journey is a matter of considerable importance for the salesman, his company and the customers. The basis of most efficiently conducted operations is that they have been well planned in advance and that care has been taken to try to foresee as many eventualities as possible.

It is impossible to plan to meet every situation but the preparation and planning which is done carefully in advance will minimize the risk of an operation becoming wasteful.

As with all operations, planning a sales journey reduces the risk of mistakes and increases the chances of success. For example, a haphazard selection of customers without any thought, might easily bring the salesman face to face with some of the following situations:

Buyer not available because of early closing day.
Buyer not available because he always holds a meeting on this day.
Buyer on holiday.
Calls too far apart to complete in one day.
Call made too soon after previous call to be of value.
Loss of time because an unfamiliar route is followed.
Poor presentation because no preparation has been made for each
    buyer's individual needs.

All these situations can cause a loss of time for the salesman, reduce his chance of getting orders and in some cases irritate the buyers. A salesman who does not plan his journey and calls haphazardly on buyers at irregular intervals can scarcely expect to inculcate a regular buying habit. The impression he will give to the buyer is one of irregularity, unreliability and lack of interest in the buyer's business. Even when the salesman sells capital goods and may not expect a repeat order for several years it is probably worth his while to keep up a regular contact. By doing this he shows his continued interest and may get further business if the customer's prosperity expands and he may also receive recommendations to other potential customers.

Any salesman who has doubts about the efficacy of planning his calls and routes should, for a few days, keep an approximate record of the time he spends face to face with buyers. It may come as a surprise to find that, very often, as little as twenty per cent of his time is spent face to face with buyers. Even the time spent in front of a buyer is rarely one hundred per cent useful. Part of the interviewing time may be occupied by interruptions on the telephone or by the buyer's staff or by some social conversation started by the buyer.

Some salesmen spend a higher proportion of their time with buyers but very few of those who have to travel more than one quarter or one half of a mile between calls are able to record that half of their working time is spent face to face with buyers. The majority of travelling salesmen come into this category and it is a sobering reflection that their livelihood has to be gained in often as little as a quarter of their working day.

There are many practical difficulties in the way of increasing the effective selling time. The density of traffic, road improvement schemes, difficulties in finding space to park a car, the time which often has to be spent waiting for a buyer and the distance between calls, are only some of the hazards which can be encountered. These difficulties are usually the cause of more than half the salesman's time being spent away from customers.

Much of the wasted time is inevitable but the salesman who is industrious and ambitious and who regularly checks the proportion of his effective selling time will be keen and anxious to improve his own performance.

The advantages of planning calls and routes can often be measured in the increased volume of sales which result. Planning brings an objective into each day's work and sets the salesman a performance yardstick. A planned journey is usually less tiring because the salesman can concentrate his energies on making calls and not dissipate it on working out where the next call should be made.

The individual consideration of each customer which is necessary when making a journey plan enables the salesman to allow adequate time for each call.

Frequency of Calls

The most essential requirement in journey planning is probably the frequency of call which it is desirable to maintain. Sometimes the salesman may have a fixed journey cycle laid down by his Sales Manager. The journey cycle may be rigid and the salesman provided each week with a list of customers on whom he should call and, perhaps, copy invoices and statements of accounts for collection. When a salesman has no precise instructions but is expected to 'sales manage' his own territory the journey plan which he makes will probably be based on the desirable frequency of call.

Each customer should be considered individually and a number of factors applied to each. The important ones are:

1 *The size and importance of the customer.*

The size refers to size of turnover in the type of goods sold by the salesman as, obviously, the higher the turnover, the more interesting the customer becomes. Customers who are big buyers usually expect to be called upon regularly.

Importance is not always related to the size of the turnover.

Although customers with high turnovers are important there are often some customers who buy comparatively small amounts but yet are important contacts. This often arises when sales are made to a research establishment. The results of the researches may affect substantially the subsequent sales to the industries for which the research is carried out and the salesman should realize the importance of close contact with research establishments. Occasionally, quite small customers have considerable influence because the buyer or proprietor holds voluntary office in a trade or professional association.

2   *The rate of stock turn of the goods.*

In the case of users the rate of stock turn would be the rate of usage. Associated closely is the ordering frequency of customers. It may be necessary to call on customers as frequently as once per week but this is unusual except for wholesalers' salesmen. The rate of stock turn and ordering frequency does not necessarily mean that a salesman should be available each time the buyer wishes to order but he needs to maintain regular contact when the order frequency is high so that he is constantly aware of the performance of his goods. Often the buying of goods for replacement is the responsibility of a storekeeper or warehouseman and a buyer has to be seen when there are variations in specifications or new products to be introduced. The storekeeper or warehouseman should be seen frequently and the salesman should also make regular but, perhaps, less frequent contact with the buyer.

3   *The frequency of call desired by the buyer.*

If the buyer decides that he wishes the salesman to call at a stated frequency and this, is a reasonable request then obviously the salesman should accede to the demand.

4   *The stock levels held by the customer.*

The level of stocks held can be an important factor in deciding the frequency of call and care should be taken to allow for the effect on stocks of seasonal fluctuations. When considering this factor the salesman should remember that if he calls when the customer is out of stock, he may be too late. The assessment of stocks levels and the estimate of the most opportune time to call can play a considerable part in getting orders in some trades.

5   *Early closing days.*

This factor and the related one of buyers' special days and times for interviewing salesmen are not major factors in deciding the frequency of call but, obviously, they must be allowed for when choosing the days and the times on which calls must be made. It is useful to maintain records of this kind of information.

6   *The number of people to be seen at each call.*

On some occasions the salesman may have to see a storeman or several storemen before he contacts the buyer. There can be far greater complications when selling components to industry because several different departments may be involved. It may be necessary to consult the design, research, production and buying departments before the specification can be agreed. When the specification has been agreed the salesman may have to submit samples for test before finally getting the order. Allowance has to be made when planning a journey for the time which needs to be spent at each call.

7   *Time for prospection.*

Every salesman should try to spend some time looking for new business and an allowance needs to be made when planning the journey so that prospection time can be included. However, the salesman should exercise a sense of responsibility and remember that obtaining new customers is not necessarily in the best interests of either his own company or his other customers. For example, products of an exclusive nature are enhanced when sold through specialist or selective outlets and any new accounts opened should justify themselves in terms of profitability.

Each of the factors enumerated should be considered for each customer and a call value given. A call value denotes the frequency, usually in weeks, at which a customer should be seen. A call value of 1, for example, would mean a weekly call, and 5 would mean a call once every five weeks. When call values have been allotted to each customer a simple list can be made as follows:

10 *customers*	*with a call value of*					1
20 "	"	"	"	"	"	2
50 "	"	"	"	"	"	3
100 "	"	"	"	"	"	4
200 "	"	"	"	"	"	5

380 *customers*

The longest time which should elapse between calls is five weeks and the journey should, therefore, be completed in this time. The salesman can now work out the total number of calls which he will have to make within each five-week journey period.

Calls

10	customers	to	be seen	each	week	for	5	wks	is	10×5		= 50
20	"	"	"	"	every	2 wks	"	5	"	"	$20 \times 2\frac{1}{2}$	= 50
50	"	"	"	"	"	3	"	"	5	"	"	$50 \times 1\frac{2}{3}$	= 83
100	"	"	"	"	"	4	"	"	5	"	"	$100 \times 1\frac{1}{4}$	= 125
200	"	"	"	"	"	5	"	"	5	"	"	200×1	= 200

508

On this basis the salesman should make 102 calls each week or a fraction over 20 calls per day in a five-day working week. This may or may not be possible according to the time which has to be spent with each customer, the size of the salesman's territory and the distance between calls. The example quoted could refer to an urban area where the salesman calls on the grocery trade. In this example no time has been allowed for prospection and it might be necessary to extend the time between calls for some of the customers. The extension of the journey cycle from five to six or seven weeks without altering the call values would not make any significant difference to the number of calls per week or the time available for prospection. To make time available the call values would have to be altered by, say, moving some customers from the categories of 2 to 3, 3 to 4 or 4 to 5.

Location

The location of customers must, obviously, have an important bearing on the journey plan. The simple rule is the shortest distance between calls but several of the factors which were considered in deciding the frequency of call will prevent the simple rule being followed exactly.

As a general rule the closest proximity between calls should govern the order in which customers are seen. This must, however, be modified by the call value and other considerations.

It is a good plan for the salesman to use a fairly large-scale map of his area and to plot the location of his customers. If customers with different call values can be distinguished by using different coloured pins or differently coloured ink crosses, the marking will be more purposeful. When the locations have been marked the salesman can see at a glance where his customers are situated and can see where the more important customers with low call values lie in relation to his other customers.

The map, complete with marked locations, can be used to plot routes so that, whenever possible, the principle of closest proximity can be followed. It is helpful when making up the journey to do so by building it up in one-day 'blocks'. Since each customer should be considered individually and early closing days, a buyer's special buying times and the call values taken into account, the actual day of the week usually has to be chosen to suit these requirements.

When a salesman has a number of important customers with low call values who have to be seen at shorter intervals, the value of selecting a suitable day is more apparent. If the salesman plans his calling routine so that he sees his important customers, and as many of the others as possible, on the same day each time, and at approximately the same time, he should be able to inculcate a regular buying habit. The buyer who sees a salesman every Monday afternoon at about 3 p.m. begins to expect him and sometimes has an order ready.

By examining the map closely the salesman should be able to form a rough idea of groups of customers which will make up a day's work. It does not matter if the number of calls is low, because the extra time may be used for prospection. When a rough journey list of customers has been made up in a series of 'days of work' it is helpful to superimpose a grid over the map. The example given below is rectangular but very rarely will a salesman's area be an exact rectangle, neither will each day nor each week be made up of geographical rectangles. The shape of each geographical 'day's work' will obviously depend on the location of the customers.

In Table 3.1, a five-day working week has been used and a four-week journey cycle. This gives the salesman twenty working days before he repeats the same journey. Each working day should be about equal so that prospection time is available in all localities unless there are known areas which require special prospection.

It will be seen that on Day 6 the salesman is back near the area covered on Day 1. By following this system the salesman can call back with the minimum of inconvenience on those buyers with a call value of one and on any buyers who happened not to be available on the previous occasion.

Table 3.1

Day 1	Day 2	Day 3	Day 4	Day 5
6	7	8	9	10
11	12	13	14	15
16	17	18	19	20

Each day's work follows in turn geographically but it will need modification to accommodate early closing days and the other factors mentioned earlier. The grid is only a guide to ensure regular and systematic coverage and to facilitate calling back.

If there is a considerable number of customers with low call values the grid may not be entirely suitable because on say, Day 16, the salesman may have to travel back over the areas covered on Days 11, 6 and 1. This can waste time and cause considerable inconvenience.

Sometimes when an area is based on one large town, with the surrounding country as part of the territory, a segmented circle can be used as a basis for journey planning. This method may benefit from the common situation that many towns or cities have main roads constructed on a radial pattern leading from the city centre like the spokes of a wheel. As often happens the more important customers with low call values may be mainly sited near the city centre or its immediate vicinity. If the journey plan is constructed with each day being an approximate segment of the circle the salesman can see his important customers each day by either starting in the centre or ending his day's work there and the main routes may facilitate travel. Figure 3.1 illustrates the principle and, as in the earlier example, is based on a five-day week and a four-weekly journey cycle with each day numbered.

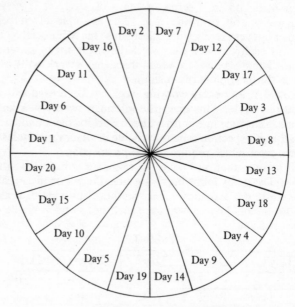

Figure 3.1 Journey Plan

The segmented circle, like the grid, is only a guide and very rarely will a salesman's territory be ideal for either system but the basis of each may be used to help construct the journey plan.

When the journey plan has been made it should be tried out in practice before any amendments are incorporated so that the salesman has the opportunity of testing its value. Usually amendments have to

be made because of the difficulty in gauging, from a map, which roads
are the most suitable to use.

Profitability

Every salesman should be interested in the profitability of his own
operations because his success is very much dependent upon this
factor. Few salesmen are given precise costs of their own operational
expenses but most of them can make an estimate which should be
reasonably accurate. The costs which they can estimate are their own
direct operating expenses and will not include the overhead costs of
supervision and administration of the sales force. The items to include
are:

  Salary
  Commission
  Bonuses
  Direct expenses including hotels, travelling, car expenses, enter-
  tainment, etc.
  Estimate of the insurance, taxation and depreciation of car.

When the salesman has estimated his total annual direct costs he
should divide this down to a weekly basis and then down to the
average cost per call. He should be able to do this quite easily by
dividing his total weekly costs by the average number of calls which he
makes each week.

By working out his approximate cost per call the salesman gets a
realistic appreciation of his costs and can relate the value of an
individual customer's turnover to the cost incurred. With this in mind
the salesman can consciously assess the value of the time that he is
spending on each call and can judge the merits of each case
realistically. Difficulties may arise when the salesman is seeking new
business as he may find it hard to make an estimate of the potential
business to be gained. It should, however, encourage him to make a
realistic appraisal of potential customers.

In considering the economy of operation the salesman should
examine his journey plan to see if there are any improvements which
can be made which will improve his profitability. The examination
should cover the following aspects:

1 *The value of each customer's business.*
   If the value in terms of profitability to the salesman's company is
   examined it may be found worthwhile to give up calling on some
   customers or to change the call value so that more attention can be
   given to prospection for new business.
2 *Delays due to traffic.*
   It may be possible to travel by a different route or different means

of transport which will save time and permit extra calls to be made.
3 *The routes used.*
Most car drivers are constantly seeking short cuts or less congested
routes and the salesman may find ways of saving time in travel by
using a different route.
4 *Delays on buyers' premises.*
Delays of this nature may be unavoidable but an attempt to avoid
them may be successful. Some buyers will be willing to make
definite appointments by telephone and this can save considerable
time. Often buyers only start to examine their stocks after a
salesman arrives and delays occur whilst stock cards are consulted,
warehousemen questioned or sometimes the stock physically
examined and counted. If the salesman can persuade buyers to do
this work before he arrives a considerable amount of time can be
saved.
5 *Social conversation.*
A salesman should never be unsociable but he should always
remember that while pleasant social conversation can smoothe the
path to an order, it should be kept to a reasonable proportion of the
selling time. The best time to be sociable is when the salesman has
obtained the order and can use sociability as the prelude to a
graceful departure. Many salesmen have expressed the view that
the ability to take an interest in a buyer's personal hobbies is the
best asset that a salesman can have. In a highly competitive
commercial market this view is scarcely tenable. The salesman can
be sociable and businesslike and by being so he is likely to win the
respect of his buyers. The businesslike salesman usually
represents a businesslike firm and buyers, as a rule, recognize the
connection.
6 *The first and last calls.*
The salesman should review the times of his first and last calls. Can
an earlier start and a later finish be made? By extending his times
of operation extra calls can be included in a day's work and extra
business is more likely to result.
7 *The sales presentation.*
The sales presentation for different selling points and advantages
of the product can be examined critically to see if any irrelevancies
have been included. Very often the impact of a sales presentation is
improved by making it shorter and more easily understood. This
may not only save time but may also help to get more orders.
8 *Timing.*
Few salesmen are clock watchers in the sense that they stop work
at a given hour. But a salesman should be conscious of time. If he
knows the time taken between calls and the time spent with each

customer he can develop the ability to plan his interviews to cover a given time span. No salesman should be too rigid about time but an awareness of a schedule and a planned number of calls per day will sharpen his perception of the task in hand.

In considering profitability the salesman should look at a wider horizon than his operating expenses and the efficiency of his methods of working. He should also examine his sales. The degree of profitability on the different products which he sells may vary considerably. If his management has not advised him which are the lines that are most profitable he should enquire. Certain lines may show a higher profit margin and certain classes of trade may be more profitable than others.

It is well worth the salesman's attention to try to eliminate unnecessary expenses such as special enquiries for modified products. The unusual orders often referred to as 'one-off jobs' are, as a rule, expensive to make and show a lower margin of profit. If it is in the company's interest to concentrate on certain lines in the range so that the volume of sales and the unit cost can be reduced the salesman should try to influence sales in this direction.

Queries from customers can be additional items of expenses and the salesman should always try to settle them personally so that delays and unnecessary correspondence are avoided.

Prospection

The two basic requirements for undertaking prospection are a sound product knowledge, which enables the salesman to recognize the opportunities to sell his product, and the time for doing prospection. To these two requirements should be added the resource and initiative of the salesman and his diligence in seeking out new business.

Prospection is not limited to the finding of new customers but also includes ways of persuading existing customers to increase sales of the lines which they handle and to stock additional lines.

Once a salesman has opened an account his objective should be to increase his sales to the customer and to extend the range of products stocked. Success with one product may be followed by successes with others and no opportunity should be missed to introduce new lines which may reasonably be bought by the customer.

The sources which a salesman can use to help him find new customers may vary between industries but the following suggestions can be applied to most trades.

1   *His own observations.*
    The salesman should be constantly on the alert and should make a mental note and a written one, if necessary, of any possible lead.

The names of premises passed on journeys to customers and the names on lorries or vans can often lead to new business.

2   *Trade directories.*

Most trades and industries have directories and these are available, as a rule, in the reference libraries of most medium and large boroughs. An examination may reveal the existence of additional and hitherto unknown prospects. Directories are not, however, always complete and sometimes only contain the names and addresses of those firms in the trade or industry which are members of the trade association which publishes the directory.

3   *The classified telephone directory.*

This source may not be as well indexed as a trade directory and may only give a general background to the trade or industry of the firms concerned. It may be more valuable in that all the firms engaged in the trade or industry are likely to be listed. Lists compiled from this source may have to be checked by a prospection call on each firm to make sure that each is engaged in the particular sphere which interests the salesman.

4   *Associated industries.*

There may be some industries which are closely associated with those to which sales are being made. Examples are the motor and aircraft industries which provide outlets for many similar products such as window frames, seat brackets, upholstery, carpets and many other items. In the food trade it is noticeable that many butchers and greengrocers are handling more grocery products. The larger self-service stores and supermarkets often stock proprietary medicines, hardware and ladies hosiery and many other products which are rarely to be found in the urban grocery shops.

5   *Industries not directly associated but using similar processes.*

There are many processes which are common to dissimilar industries. A simple example is that estate agents and iron smelters may both use identical office equipment and stationery. Processes which are more unusual are paper-making equipment which is very similar to the machinery used in parts of the viscose industry, canning equipment which is used for paints and peas and labelling machinery which is widely used in many different industries.

6   *Visits to trade and technical exhibitions.*

Exhibitions may only be held in certain large centres of population but if the opportunity occurs it is often well worth the time to visit them. Many of the stands of exhibiting companies have abundant supplies of literature which give comprehensive information on the products and services which are offered. An examination of these can sometimes reveal possible sources of new business.

7 *Research departments.*
Many trades and industries have joint research organizations which undertake co-operative research for the benefit of the industry concerned. Contact with such establishments may bring to light possible new uses or developments which can be investigated. These establishments may be visited by Head Office staff and the salesman should check that he is not duplicating an existing contact.

8 *Training Schools.*
There are numerous schools throughout the country which teach tradesmen. Some are sponsored by trades or industries, others are part of the government supported technical colleges. Within this category would come the medical schools in the teaching hospitals. Schools are usually not large buyers or important in the economic sense but they can be of considerable value if a constant stream of students becomes familiar with a product that has been used during the training. When the students are qualified they may become influential and their advice on the products to be bought and used may sway buyers' opinions.

9 *Examination of competitive methods.*
The method of operation by competitors and the kind of trade which they conduct can provide a lead to new opportunities which a salesman may have overlooked. A salesman should always be on the look-out to see where competitive supplies are used.

10 *Customer recommendations.*
A recommendation from a satisfied customer to a prospect is a most valuable lead and salesmen should try to secure such recommendations as a matter of course. In some trades this may be unwise because of exclusiveness or keen competition and the salesman must use his discretion.

11 *Contact with Chambers of Commerce and Local Trade Associations.*
Organizations such as these often have permanent officials who are knowledgeable about the local conditions and the firms which are engaged in various industries. These officials may not always reveal lists of firms but a tactful approach can, on some occasions, bring worthwhile results.

12 *Examination of trade and technical magazines and the general press.*
Frequently, useful lists of prospects can be culled from the advertisement pages of trade and technical magazines. Salesmen cannot spend a lot of time reading papers in the hope of finding prospects but often such magazines are available in the waiting rooms of their customers and can be perused whilst waiting for the buyer.

13 *Enquiries from Head Office.*

A common way of providing lists of prospects is by inserting an advertisement which offers a brochure. The brochure is sent and the salesman is asked to make a follow-up call.

14 *The policeman or the postman.*

This may seem an odd heading for prospection but a friendly policeman or- postman can render very valuable aid. A representative covering a new area may have his map marked with differently coloured pins or crosses compiled from records that have been handed to him. This can be done by using indexed street maps but it only records those customers who are known and it does not find prospects. If the policeman or postman is asked if he will be kind enough to point out areas where there are shops or offices or any other kind of trade in which the salesman is interested, much time can be saved. If the kind of customers which the salesman seeks are unlikely to be congregated together or identified so easily this advice may not be valuable, but it is often worth the effort.

No matter what sources the salesman uses to find his prospects he must use his initiative and judgment firstly in finding and arousing the prospect's attention, and secondly, in appraising the business potential.

The Importance of Planning and Prospection

Good journey planning brings a sense of purpose to the salesman's work and, of course, improves his efficiency.

The main point to remember is that good planning is the result of careful investigation into the buying habits of customers, customers' locations and the cost of making calls. Although business-getting needs to be considered over a period of time – short periods for fast selling consumer goods and longer periods for durables and capital items – the salesman should not lose sight of his cost per call in relation to the value of the business obtained.

Journey planning should almost always make provision for time for prospection. Having planned his journey, the salesman is better prepared to plan his sales interviews.

4 The Sales Interview

During the sales interview the salesman can develop the use of the tools of salesmanship. These were described in an earlier chapter as Personality, Knowledge, Judgment and the Power of Persuasion. These tools need to be used regularly if they are to be developed and to be effective. The Personality and Knowledge may diminish in their power if they are not exercised regularly and a salesman's Judgment and Power of Persuasion may atrophy if they remain unused for any length of time.

To understand the sales interview fully the salesman should spend some time giving thought to how an interview is formed. The interview can be divided into five sections and an understanding of each is essential if the salesman is to make full use of the time that he spends with the buyer. Each section merits a separate and thorough study because, although each interview may be said to follow a set form, the length and combination of the five parts can vary so much that any attempt to follow a rule book slavishly is almost sure to fail.

There is an immense difference between the short sharp interview where the buyer demands to know the salesman's business and then gives a brusque 'No' and the interview where the buyer's interest has been aroused, a demonstration has been given and an order booked. Each of these interviews has had a beginning, a period during which the product could have been presented and an ending. The resemblance between them ends there; one interview failed and the other was a success.

The five parts which make up an interview are:

Preparation.
The Approach.
The Demonstration and Presentation.
Negotiation.
The Close.

Every interview should be made up of these component parts but, since an interview pattern cannot be followed slavishly, the salesman must be ready at all times to shorten any stage and move on to the next one. On occasions he may have to return to an earlier stage. For this reason it is important that each step should be studied thoroughly because, although the steps are part of a sequence, each step may achieve such significance that it becomes, on occasions, the most important part of the interview. The buyer may decide to buy at any time during the interview and the salesman should recognize this and be prepared to act accordingly.

Preparation

Every interview really starts some time before the salesman ever meets the buyer. The salesman who does not give thought to preparation before he meets the buyer is reducing his chances of success. Preparation in advance of the interview is one step towards increasing the chances of success and the salesman should take all possible steps to improve his chances.

There is probably a wealth of information available in the company records about individual buyers and the salesman should study these very carefully. There are also the records which the salesman should keep and there is often the knowledge gained from previous calls upon the buyer.

It does not matter which of the sources of information a salesman uses provided that he obtains as much information as possible about the buyer and the proposed interview. It is also important to get the information sufficiently far in advance to be able to use it intelligently.

The information which a salesman will find useful to have in advance of an interview will vary according to the type of sales methods which are used. The following suggestions are a guide which will help in most cases.

The name and status of the buyer.

It is obviously an advantage to be able to address the buyer by his name. It is also very helpful if the salesman knows the status of the buyer. He may be the proprietor, or a director with a financial interest; he may be a professional buyer with years of experience. He may be an executive of the company with a job unrelated to buying who has had the responsibility given to him. Many buyers of office stationery, for example, are company secretaries and often this type of product is bought by the shorthand-typist or secretary to the proprietor of a business.

The most suitable times for interviews.

Many buyers have specified times for seeing salesmen and attempts to obtain an interview outside these hours can cause irritation. Such buyers often have other responsibilities and have to allocate time in order to plan their own work and the salesman should respect these rules. Even when a buyer does not have special buying times it is helpful if the salesman can find out the times which are likely to be convenient and those which may be inconvenient. Often buyers have weekly meetings with their own salesmen and there may be similar calls on their time.

A record of previous purchases, payments, returns and credit rating.

It is often impossible and impracticable for the salesman to have a complete record of a buyer's purchases. The range of goods offered by the salesman may be too wide for a record to be kept. He should, however, keep a summary and be able to discuss previous purchases and the history of business transactions intelligently. If a complete record of transactions can be maintained easily this should be done and the salesman should consult the record before each call. Particular note should be made of the increases and decreases in orders of the different products which are offered so that reasons for the fluctuations can be investigated. Awareness of the credit rating of the customer is of considerable importance.

The buyer's main interests in business and social life.

Identification of the buyer's main interests in his business is important to ensure that the salesman's presentation is relevant personally. An interest in the buyer's social life should be handled with care. Some buyers prefer to keep their social life separate from their business life whilst others are happy to mix them. The salesman should be careful not to intrude and an artificial interest in a buyer's hobby can often lead to a false relationship.

The buyer's real needs.

These are often confused with a buyer's interests but care should be taken to draw a distinction between the two. The difference can be illustrated by the following example. A young man with a wife and two or three children may wish to own a sports car with a high performance and this may be his main interest. His real need is probably for a family car and, unless he indulges his interests, it is more probable that he will buy the family car. This kind of situation is constantly arising and the salesman must not only learn to draw the distinction but he must also be able to assess the importance of each.

The kind of competitive products which the buyer has purchased and his buying policy.

A background of information of the buying habits of the buyer is an important guide for the salesman. It may help him to decide whether to offer a de-luxe model or a standard model. A knowledge of the past purchases of competitive products also helps the salesman in forming his sales presentation. He should know the strengths and weaknesses of competitive products and be prepared to frame his sales arguments in the most effective way.

Any likely objections which the buyer may raise.

Forewarned is forearmed as far as objections are concerned but the salesman cannot usually hope to have much advance information in this direction. If he is fortunate enough to know in advance about possible objections then he can marshal the evidence and prepare his methods of dealing with them.

The buyer's personality and character.

Every salesman should remember that as far as personality and character are concerned it is the reaction between individuals which will count. Advance information about personality and character from a third party should always be treated with caution and the salesman should form his own judgment; the buyer may react differently to the salesman's personality. If information of this nature is available it can be helpful but the salesman should have reservations about it and should not rely upon it too heavily before forming his own judgment.

The selling points of his own product and the sales arguments.

This information is obviously of prime importance. Without it the salesman cannot operate in normal competitive times. It is also very helpful to have a thorough knowledge of competing products and the competitive sales arguments.

The organization of the buyer's business.

This kind of information is of a general character and may be helpful in interpreting the actions and demands of the buyer. There may also be helpful associations with other companies and it may be possible for the salesman to obtain worthwhile introductions.

Apart from finding out as much as possible in advance of the interview the salesman should be very careful to put his own house in order. He should make sure that he is adequately equipped with sufficient samples, literature, price lists, display material and, of course, order forms. If he carries a demonstration kit he should make sure in advance of the interview that it is in good working order and that he has any tools that are necessary in case of a breakdown and also that he has an adequate supply of any material which the machine may use during the demonstration.

With a sound background of information a salesman can plan the interview. He will know the competitive situation and may be able to judge which problems are likely to arise. He can prepare his sales arguments well in advance and, with a knowledge of the buyer's personality and character, always provided he has gained this knowledge first hand, he can decide how to present his case most effectively.

In the difficult cases where a salesman finds obstacles in the way of getting an interview with the buyer the kind of information set out above can be of considerable help. For example, a message giving details of a special selling feature or economy point which the salesman knows is likely to appeal to a particular buyer will often gain an interview which had previously been refused. When the buyer is unknown and there is no information available and an interview has been refused a similar message may also gain admission but the salesman has to take a chance as to whether his message will appeal to the buyer.

The Approach

The moment two people meet they register a mental impression upon each other and this impression may have to be reversed or changed before the two people can begin to get on with each other.

It is of extreme importance that the salesman should try to make a good first impression because an impression once made is difficult to change.

Sometimes the salesman may enlist the help of his wife, or a colleague who will give him a frank opinion on his appearance. If he decides to be self critical the points which want special attention are cleanliness of person and clothes, particularly linen. He should be neat and tidy and avoid frayed cuffs and his suit should be well pressed and brushed regularly. Extremes of fashion, unless relevant to the trade in which the salesman is engaged, should be avoided. Many buyers look at the hands and particularly the nails of people whom they meet; many also look at the shoes and mentally register an impression if those worn by the salesman are down at heel and dirty.

The salesman should also take account of his appearance as a person. It is not enough to be neat, tidy and well groomed; if the salesman has a superior manner and a permanently ill-tempered look about him he will obviously upset most people. He should cultivate a pleasant appearance and try to look as though he is genuinely pleased to see the buyer.

In the first few seconds of the interview the salesman should try to set the tone. The opening remarks contribute towards the first impression which the salesman creates.

If the buyer and the salesman are well known to each other the opening remarks will probably be both personal and friendly and the interview will get off to a good start. The interview is probably almost a continuation of the previous interview and the conversation may start where the previous one ended. This is a good relationship for a salesman to have with a buyer because he has probably inculcated a buying habit and developed a brand of loyalty which makes the business relationship a sound one.

When the buyer is not well known to the salesman or is a complete stranger the salesman must immediately try to establish a pleasant and relaxed atmosphere. The first few minutes of an interview between strangers are important, each individual is sizing up the other and there is probably a slight air of tension.

A good technique for the salesman to follow is to make some agreeable and pleasant general remark which refers to the business.

The remark should not be provocative as, although starting an interview with an argument will undoubtedly grip the buyer's attention, it is unlikely to benefit the salesman.

Examples of the kind of general opening remark are:

'I noticed on my way in, that you had an attractive window display featuring . . . '

'Your workshop looks very busy . . . '

'I'd like briefly to tell you about the products which I am selling and then answer any questions which you may wish to ask'.

'Before I tell you about my products you don't mind if I ask you a few questions so that I can save your time by mentioning only the type of products which are most suitable for your needs'.

The kind of opening remarks which a salesman makes will obviously depend upon his judgment of the buyer and may be influenced by the buyer's own conversation. If the buyer starts off by saying 'I'm a busy man, you can have five minutes, now what do you want?' the salesman must react accordingly. In this case, he may pointedly look at his watch and say, 'Right, Mr Blank, I'll just tell you the main points and show you our best selling line'. It may be advisable to make an appointment to return at a more convenient time. If a time limit is placed on the duration of the interview by the buyer, the salesman should keep to it and politely offer to go when the time is up. If the salesman has handled the situation well, it is almost certain that the buyer will grant an extension of time because he is sufficiently interested in the proposition.

During the approach period of the interview the salesman should try to make a good initial impression and should endeavour to establish the real needs of the buyer. He should check any information about the buyer and the buyer's needs which he has obtained previously so that he is up to date and has accurate information. The request for information can be made tactfully as a necessary step in the buyer's own interests.

The last stage of the approach is to arouse the buyer's interest sufficiently for the salesman to proceed to the next stage of the interview. A good way to do this is by mentioning some of the claims that are made on behalf of the product.

Whenever possible the claims should be demonstrably true or backed by independent evidence. Authenticity is personal and real for claims which the buyer can witness himself or which have the backing of independent evidence. Such evidence may be from Market Research reports which have been published or comparative tests published in technical or trade papers. Claims which cannot be substantiated should not be made because they tend to sow the seeds of doubt in a buyer's mind.

Many salesmen have to collect money from their customers and this can be used as a basis for the approach when the buyer is also responsible for the payment of accounts. After the general opening remarks the salesman can produce his copy invoice or statement and his receipt book and place them prominently in front of the buyer. As he opens his receipt book he can make a casual enquiry such as, 'Your account stands at £x. Do you prefer to pay by cheque or cash?'

The collection of money is a businesslike way of opening an interview because it clears the liability of the buyer and is often a natural way of obtaining a further order, particularly for repeat selling goods.

The Demonstration and Presentation

Where there is a product to be demonstrated the salesman should have made himself an efficient operator in the technical sense. The product should be carefully examined and the major selling points and advantages over competitors' products should be listed. The method of demonstrating should be planned so that the major selling points and advantages are clearly placed before the customer. In demonstrating, it is usually of considerable value if a planned sequence is followed. The plan should be simple and the sequence of operations should be in a logical order.

The salesman should preface the demonstration with a simple explanation of the principle by which the product works, how it operates and the results which can be expected. This brief background serves as an introduction and is designed to prepare the ground for a more detailed explanation. During the explanation the various features of the product can be shown so that the buyer gets to know something about it before the actual demonstration starts. The reason for taking so much trouble before the demonstration starts is that very few buyers or operatives can absorb the principles by which a product functions at the same time as they watch it in action. When, for example, a machine is in operation there is often a noise but there is always the distraction of the machine at work and the salesman has to compete with the machine for the buyer's attention.

After the opening explanation the salesman should then explain the sequence of the operation and, if it is possible, go through the sequence before giving the actual demonstration.

Finally, the salesman should give the demonstration himself. The time and effort taken before the actual demonstration may seem laborious but it fulfils an important function. The principles and the working of the product have been explained without any distractions and during this time the salesman has had the opportunity to familiarize himself with his surroundings. Any adjustments that may be necessary can be made before the demonstration takes place and any potential operatives who may have been invited to the demonstration will have been given a thorough explanation.

When the salesman has given his demonstration he should then invite the buyer or operatives to use the machine or product so that they can experience the advantages themselves. The salesman should always try to avoid allowing his customer to use the machine or product first. So often mistakes in handling an unfamiliar piece of equipment can happen and the demonstration may fail.

The sequence in demonstrating a product plays an important part in making the demonstration a success and for easy reference the recommended sequence is summarized.

1 Explain the principles of the machine or product.
2 Give the sequence of operation with any explanations.
3 Give the demonstration.
4 Let the customer use the product.

Giving a demonstration is a very helpful way of making sales because the buyer has his attention drawn to the product in operation often on his own premises. Whenever a salesman has a chance to give a demonstration he should always seize the opportunity.

Many salesmen sell products which cannot be demonstrated in the same way as, say office equipment or tools. Those salesmen who sell services such as office and factory maintenance and cleaning have nothing tangible to show or demonstrate. These salesmen should use the same techniques but adapt them to their products. This can be done in the following manner.

Firstly, the salesman should explain how the service came into operation to fill a need. Most buyers will probably have the same need if the salesman has done his prospecting thoroughly. Then the salesman should pass naturally to an explanation of how his service meets the need. The demonstration part now follows by the adaptation of the service to the buyer's individual needs and by tactful question and answer the buyer begins to understand how the service can operate in his business.

Similarly the techniques can be adopted for selling inanimate goods but often even inanimate goods can be 'demonstrated' by tests such as tasting, wearing, attempted destruction or application.

When presenting his products to a buyer whether or not they can be demonstrated the salesman should remember the analysis of the advantages, benefits and disadvantages which should be listed against the main buying interests of Performance, Economy, Durability, Appearance, Safety, Comfort, Adaptability, Publicity support, Distribution and Service.

It is during the demonstration and presentation that the buyer becomes interested in the advantages and the benefits to him. The salesman should always try to relate the advantages and benefits to the buyer's individual needs. At this stage of the interview the salesman should be utilizing the information which he has gained during the approach stage of the interview.

Examples of how the advantages and benefits may be related to individual needs are:

'In a shop like yours our experience shows that you will probably sell one gross of our biscuits every fourteen days. With our quick delivery service you will be able to turn over your stock at least every two weeks and so have twenty-six opportunities every year of making a profit on the capital employed.'

The use of estimated profit figures will make this kind of argument personal and realistic.

'If you buy this high quality material you will have fewer machine stoppages, less wastage and a better quality finish to your product'.

Negotiation

In some trades the salesman does not negotiate because he is selling a nationally advertised branded good which may have a fixed price to the trade. The prices and terms may be laid down as part of company policy, the carriage paid minimum quantity may be specified and the salesman's activities are concerned mainly with selling and display.

Many salesmen, however, have to negotiate on price, product specification, selling rights, delivery times and perhaps other points. Whether or not a salesman has to negotiate, it is very much worth his while to study the methods of negotiation in case the need should ever arise.

Negotiation is usually defined as 'conferring with another with the view to compromise or agree on some issue'. The first principle which a salesman must have clear in his mind is the precise limits within which he is allowed to negotiate. Unless he is clear about these limits his negotiations may be repudiated or accepted with loss. The salesman should get from his management the precise details of the price brackets which he can use, the specifications which he can quote, the extent of the exclusiveness which he can offer and the expected delivery times. If there are any other points on which he will be expected to negotiate he should find the precise limits of his authority.

The second principle is to form an estimate of the buyer's precise needs. This requires very tactful questioning, acute observation and as much knowledge of the buyer and his business as possible. It is helpful to know the buyer's turnover of different products, his usage, the discounts which he gives if he is a distributor and the service which he renders. Sometimes the salesman can discover, quite legitimately, the price which the buyer is paying for competitors' goods. With information of this nature the salesman can begin to negotiate with confidence but negotiation without information is more difficult. Much of the knowledge of a customer's business can only be acquired through long personal contact and all information which is gleaned should be carefully noted.

When a salesman has a sound knowledge of the buyer's needs and his business he learns to distinguish the important points for negotiation and can form a judgment of the value to the buyer of the concessions which he (the salesman) can make. Many negotiations have been concluded successfully by a salesman allowing some quite minor concession to a buyer after prolonged negotiation.

The third principle in negotiation is to keep as many concessions in reserve as possible. Negotiation is bargaining and is a perfectly proper way of selling. Many people consider bargaining is confined to eastern markets but every day in the western world business is conducted by bargaining. Respectable and long-established institutions such as the Stock Exchange, Lloyds and the Commodity Markets in the City of London are daily examples where bargains are struck.

If it is the company's policy to allow their salesmen freedom, within certain limits, to negotiate prices it is the salesman's duty to obtain the best bargain that he can for his company although he should take account of the long term relationships with his customers. When conducting negotiations the salesman should allow concessions only when he is satisfied that the concession is a necessary step towards obtaining the order. Concessions should only be allowed after a thorough discussion and exploration of the value of other benefits which the buyer will enjoy regardless of the granting of the concession.

In following the three principles the salesman should use his judgment and knowledge and frame his proposals accordingly. Most salesmen, who have the power to negotiate, are paid a percentage of their turnover in commission and skill in negotiation can be very profitable.

The Close

Closing the sale often seems more difficult in prospect than it is in practice. Many salesmen think there is a psychological moment when the deal should be clinched. Undoubtedly, there are times during an interview which are more favourable for closing a sale. The salesman should be able to recognize these times but it is far more important that he should be able to create the situation when the time will be favourable.

Some salesmen are hesitant about trying to close a sale and feel that, having explained carefully to the buyer's satisfaction all that he wants to know, it is up to the buyer to place the order. These salesmen should think about their own job and consider why they are employed because the salesman's prime function is selling and he can only do this by getting orders.

The salesman should remember his role and function and, if he is satisfied that he has made a reasonable commercial proposition to the buyer, he should have no qualm about asking for an order. No salesman can expect a buyer to take him seriously, if, after spending time explaining and demonstrating a product, making claims for it and justifying them, he fails to ask for an order. Failure to ask for the order shows a lack of confidence and conviction and the buyer may be excused for thinking that the salesman has perhaps exaggerated some of his claims and is frightened of being found out.

The sales interview has been set out in the logical stages of Preparation, The Approach, Demonstration and Presentation, Negotiation and The Close. Unfortunately, it often does not follow this pattern and a buyer, for example, may demand to negotiate at the start of the interview because he thinks he has all the information he needs about the product. The salesman, therefore, should always be prepared to close and to ask for the order at any time during the interview.

Closing the sale is very much like a game of association football. The ultimate objective is an order or a goal. In selling, the discussion may range over wide issues and some of them may provide the opportunity for closing the sale. Just as in football an unexpected pass may provide the opportunity for scoring a goal. The chance has to be recognised and the opportunity taken.

Most salesmen will confess to missed opportunities and frankly admit that, at some time during their sales careers, they have talked themselves into an order and then talked themselves out of it. Fortunately, most salesmen recognise this failing early in their careers and quickly learn how to avoid it.

The first and most important thing to learn about closing sales is that the salesman must always be ready to close just as in football the players must always be ready to shoot at the goal.

The salesman who is ready must also be able to recognise the opportunities. Sometimes the opportunities are created by him and he will need no guidance in recognising them. On other occasions the opportunity may be shown by the buyer in a casual and apparently disinterested way.

Situations which offer opportunities are fairly easy to recognize because they are usually an extension of the buyer's interest. During the discussions a buyer may suddenly show further interest in the subject or express an interest in a different subject.

Signs which can herald the opportunity are:

'What delivery service do you give?'
'How soon can you deliver?'
'Can you deliver by van?'
'What colours have you?'
'Do you have a red model?'

Whenever the buyer shows an extension of interest or a sudden change of interest on any subject relative to the product the salesman should realise that the opportunity may have come.

The indications may be so clear that the salesman feels he should ask for the order and, if so, he will probably succeed. If the indications are not so precise, the salesman has an opportunity of using a trial close. This is a technique which infers that the buyer will buy but does not do so directly.

The trial close is often the start of a closing sequence which leads to the order. Very often the trial close will bring the order immediately without any further effort by the salesman. The advantages of using it are that it can bring orders, and it is not so direct that the buyer is likely to give a categorical refusal. If the buyer is not willing to buy, his answer is likely to allow the interview to continue without any hiatus being created in the buyer/salesman relationship. Finally, the trial close, when it does not get an order, usually gets an answer from which the salesman can assess the progress he is making towards the order.

Experienced salesmen are usually expert in making trial closes because they realize that these are a gradual approach to order-getting.

Examples of trial closes which can be used are:

'Which model do you think is the most useful for your type of work?'
'Which are the most popular sizes that you sell?'

'Do you prefer the black or the white colour?'

These examples are conversational enquiries with only slight inferences that an order is being sought. Other examples which can be used but which are stronger are:

'When do you think you will require delivery?'
'Would you like these made to match the set which you have?'
'I expect you will want to take advantage of our special bonus offer.'

The trial close can be used at the salesman's discretion and need not be confined to situations where the buyer has revealed an extension of interest and an opportunity for closing.

In the cases where the salesman has created the opportunities for closing he will obviously use a technique which fits in with the circumstances. There are several ways of creating a situation which can lead naturally to closing the sale. During the course of the sales interview the salesman may have established what the key issue is and, therefore, he goes to some trouble to satisfy the buyer on this point. Having satisfied the buyer on the most important issue the salesman can ask for the order without any embarrassment.

Sometimes it is difficult to establish a key issue because the buyer has expressed interest on several features of the product. In such cases the salesman should try to obtain the buyer's agreement or satisfaction about each feature. In following this method it is natural, after getting agreement or satisfaction from the buyer, to ask for the order.

Yet another way of creating a situation which can lead to a close is to discuss delivery dates, the availability of stock, special modifications which the buyer may require, or any feature which is identified personally with the buyer's individual requirements. Assent to any of these discussions can also lead to a natural request for an order. In certain circumstances the situation may be created by arousing a sense of urgency. The salesman may be able to point out that stocks are getting low, a special bonus offer is about to end or deliveries must be made quickly if the buyer wishes to meet a seasonal demand.

Before the closing stage of the interview is reached, the salesman should have satisfied the buyer's needs. It is unlikely that a successful closing technique can be used unless this is done. The subject of the analysis of the buyer's interests is dealt with in a later chapter but it should be borne in mind when considering closing techniques.

Having created a situation where the request for the order will come as a natural, logical step the salesman can use a number of ways of framing his request for it.

The simplest and most straightforward way is to ask directly for an order. This is a natural request to make if the salesman is confident that he has satisfied the buyer's needs.

One of the most common methods of asking for the order is by offering the customer an alternative choice. This method is widely used and can be adapted for all sorts of situations. Examples are:

'Would you like ten or fifteen gross?'

'Shall I send ten black and fifteen blue models or would you like a different proportion?'

'Do you prefer to take advantage of our cash discount or would you like to examine the credit terms?'

'Would you like immediate delivery or will next week be soon enough?'

The question should always be framed in a positive way and the alternatives offered must be realistic within the context of each buyer's requirements. Unrealistic alternatives are not likely to be taken seriously.

A method which can be used effectively is for the salesman to summarize the points raised by the customer and to ask him if he is satisfied with the explanations which have been given. If the answer is affirmative, the salesman proceeds on the assumption that the customer will buy and produces and starts to complete his order form.

The suggestion of a definite date for delivery is an effective way of closing and this can often be facilitated by reference to a coming event or important date in the calendar. An example is:

'You will want to get delivery in before Easter so shall I send them straightaway?'

A useful way of getting an order for some quite expensive merchandise such as a car is to sell a minor fitment that can be added. In the case of a car the issue might be decided by a question such as: 'I assume you will want us to fit registration plates for you?' The use of a minor issue tends to lessen the awesome character of a transaction and make it more acceptable.

In some trades it is possible, as a closing technique, to grant some inducement or concession which will sway the buyer. Sometimes the concession technique is used when the customer's goods are taken in part exchange and a small extra amount may be added to the trade in value which is allowed.

The buyer may sometimes be stimulated into buying if he becomes aware that one of his rivals has bought the product. This spur to a buyer has to be handled with care and the salesman should take particular trouble not to break the confidence of other customers. Another effective way is to let the buyer handle the goods and become so used to them that he develops pride of ownership.

When the salesman has closed the sale and got the order he should guard against the display of a sudden loss of interest. The buyer should be thanked politely and respectfully but not effusively. The opportunity may be taken at this time for a short social conversation as a graceful way of leaving. A salesman who leaves abruptly after getting an order displays a lack of personal interest in the buyer which may be resented.

The Interview Plan in Perspective

It is important to understand the stages in an interview but just as important to be flexible in front of the buyer and to be ready to change the plan.

The competent salesman 'thinks on his feet' but is better able to do so if his basic knowledge includes a thorough understanding of the importance of pre-interview preparation, varying techniques of the approach, how to demonstrate and present his product, the techniques of negotiation and finally, the most important of all, how to close the sale.

Closing techniques should always be affirmative, positive and confident but phrased in a friendly manner.

The psychological considerations which follow in the next chapter show some of the techniques of handling buyers and also some of the opportunities which may arise for introducing closing techniques.

5 The Psychological Considerations of Moods and Motives

In considering the psychology of selling, the salesman has two aspects to examine; himself and the buyer. In Chapter I the personality and attributes of the salesman were considered but the successful utilization of them depends on the effect which they have on buyers.

The salesman must, therefore, be able to judge how buyers will react to him as a personality and, to make effective judgments, he has to understand the personality of the various buyers with whom he conducts business.

The behaviour patterns of most intelligent people are motivated by their interests. Sometimes these interests are logical and the behaviour pattern follows empirical reasoning but on other occasions the behaviour is the result of emotions such as love and fear.

It is difficult for the salesman who is not, as a rule, a trained psychologist to trace back the origin of a buyer's decision. In any event the origin will rarely be traceable to a single cause. Most behaviour patterns are a result of people's experiences and are inextricably mixed as regards empirical reasoning and emotional interests.

The salesman has neither the training nor the time for clinical analysis and, in any event, if he exercises acute observation and makes mental notes of the buyer's reactions he will find sufficient guidance for his purpose. The most important point that a salesman should always have in his mind is that people are individuals. People vary in the make up of their personalities and resent being categorized and treated as a 'type'. A salesman who takes the trouble to treat all his buyers as individual beings will very quickly establish a rapport with them.

Apart from the wide differences between the personalities of individuals there are day-to-day variations in the individual. The saying that someone 'must have got out of the wrong side of the bed this morning' is an example of the kind of variations which everyone experiences.

Although the individual treatment of people is essential for successful salesmanship it is helpful to examine some broad types of behaviour patterns and to learn to identify, interpret and handle them.

The Interpretation of Buyers' Moods

It is rarely easy to interpret the moods of people. Most adults control their emotions and their moods and minor variations are often indiscernible except to close friends who know them well. Even when changes of emotions and moods are shown the signs which are manifest rarely identify clearly what kind of mood has taken possession of the individual. Salesmen meet all kinds of buyers and often, even in one day, there is a considerable variation in the personalities and moods of the buyers who are seen.

Some typical moods, the characteristics by which they may sometimes be recognized and general suggestions for handling them are set out in the next section.

The brusque, business-like buyer

This kind of buyer can often be recognized by his insistence on getting down to business straight away and demanding the facts. The salesman, in such cases, is often subjected almost to a cross examination. The way in which it is suggested that this buyer be handled is to be just as business-like, to have the product or samples readily available, the booklets or leaflets ready and to know all the necessary facts and data about the product.

A few business-like questions about the buyer's needs and problems will demonstrate that the salesman wishes to overcome the particular problems in a thorough and business-like manner. With such a buyer it is advisable to give just the major claims and to substantiate them.

The dictatorial buyer

Every salesman meets this kind of buyer occasionally. This type has a power complex and often likes to put salesmen at a disadvantage. Fortunately there is only a small minority of them and, although not difficult to handle, they can be unpleasant. They can be easily recognized by actions of discourtesy and intolerance. They frequently interrupt and make dogmatic statements and often treat their own staff ungraciously.

The salesman should always be relaxed and composed and should never get flustered or hurried. If a series of questions are fired at the salesman he should answer the first one thoroughly before dealing with any of the subsequent ones. If it has not been possible to remember all the questions the salesman should, without any embarrassment, ask the buyer to repeat them.

The hesitant buyer

This type of buyer is often changeable and uncertain and obviously lacks confidence. During an interview his moods may change from enthusiasm for the product to scepticism.

In such cases the salesman should present his sales arguments very clearly, using simple language and short, easy-to-follow sentences. Only the major selling points should be presented so that the buyer is not confused with too many issues.

This type of buyer really needs someone to make up his mind for him, and, if the salesman gives him a clear lead and sound advice, the buyer will come to rely upon him.

The over-familiar buyer

Sometimes salesmen encounter buyers who are very congenial and friendly and who seem to take a close interest in the product. They are good humoured and are willing to talk about sport or any other subject.

The salesman should try to join in the congenial conversation but should do his best to confine it to the business on hand. The approach, demonstration and presentation should be made pleasantly but great care should be taken not to be misled by the friendly, easy acceptance of the selling points. The use of 'trial closes' is strongly recommended during this type of interview because they will help to keep the buyer's mind on the business in hand, and, at the same time, help the salesman to assess his progress towards making the sale.

The busy buyer

Sometimes this type of buyer appears to be busy because he is ill organized. At other times the buyer will be genuinely busy because of pressure of work. It is not always easy to distinguish between the two categories particularly at a first meeting. Such buyers are usually recognizable no matter which category they belong to by their hurried movements, general air of anxiety and the difficulty of concentrating on the sales presentation because too many other issues are intruding upon their minds. A genuinely busy buyer may, however, show no trace of anxiety and only display a keenness to get on with business matters.

On these occasions the salesman should be brisk and concise and should state his sales arguments briefly but clearly. When he has presented his arguments he should check that the product satisfies the buyer's needs and should ask forthrightly for the order.

The uncommunicative buyer

The buyer who scarcely talks is a very difficult man to handle and no advice is needed on how to recognize him. The art of presenting a product depends very much on the salesman's judgment of the buyer and, if the buyer is uncommunicative, it is hard to interpret his mood or judge his personality.

The salesman should try to persuade the buyer to talk by tactfully commenting about some aspect of the business and following up his remarks with a few innocuous questions. The questions should be of a general business character but not so pertinent as to be likely to meet with a rebuff. If the buyer responds to this approach the salesman should try to draw him out and get him to help in the demonstration or take part conversationally in the presentation.

The hostile buyer

Occasionally the salesman will come across a buyer who is hostile, perhaps because of some grievance against the salesman's company in the past. Usually the hostility manifests itself in disparaging remarks about the salesman's products, his company and service.

When this type of buyer is met the salesman should be prepared to listen attentively and to take particular note of the grievance and should try to find out how it arose.

If it is within the salesman's power to right the grievance he should do so; if not, he should ask forthrightly for the opportunity of demonstrating the ability of his company to supply quality goods and to support them with satisfactory service. At all times he should be most punctilious in dealing with the customer.

These are some of the moods which salesmen encounter regularly and the suggested methods of handling such situations should be used only as a guide. The salesman should remember that it is the individual reaction between his own personality and that of the buyer which will influence the outcome of the interview.

Analysis of Main Buying Interests and Motives

The difficulties of analysing the reasons for making decisions has been mentioned but the salesman must make an attempt. During his interviews with buyers he should try to identify the main buying interests and why the particular interests are important to individual buyers.

Some buyers, because of their upbringing or commercial experience, have a slightly unbalanced attitude to the products which are offered to them. The personal bias may be towards economy, appearance or some other buying interest and has developed because it was a successful feature on some past occasion. Equally there may be a bias against some interest because of an unfortunate experience.

During his regular contact with buyers the salesman should try to identify the prejudices of his buyers. Prejudices very quickly become habits and one of the salesman's tasks is to inculcate a buying habit for his own products. He can only do this successfully if he knows the prejudices and habits of the buyer and has some understanding of how they came into being.

There are two main fields for the salesman's analysis and these are the logical reasons and the emotional reasons which motivate the buying decisions. The distinction between the two is important and the salesman should try to identify each before deciding which or what combination of both is to be used for basing his sales presentation.

Research into motives has always been regarded as necessary. Fifty years ago the salesman wanted to know 'what made the buyer tick?' Nowadays the phrase used is more likely to be 'motivation research'. A measure of the importance attached to this kind of research is that during the last few years interest in it has grown considerably. Most of the larger corporations in the United States of America use motivation research and it is a growing practice among the larger companies in the United Kingdom. It has been used by public bodies such as transport companies to determine behaviour patterns of the travelling public and has led to design modifications of public service vehicles. It has been publicly accepted by one political party and used by them for determining the behaviour pattern of the electorate.

The methods of carrying out motivation research are complex, and both psychologists and sociologists have become deeply involved. The salesman does not have the benefit of the training received by psychologists and sociologists but he has intelligence, acute observation and experience and it is these qualities which he should use to analyse motives.

The main buying interests were given in Chapter 2 and, if the salesman is to appeal to them effectively, he must be able to identify and interpret them accurately. The emotions which can motivate a buyer should also be identified and interpreted and both main buying interests and motives are analysed more fully in the following sections.

Main Buying Interests

These are the interests which generally motivate the rational behaviour of a buyer and lead him to make buying decisions.

They are usually associated with the material advantages and benefits of a product or service. It is not strictly true to say that these interests are always rational because as mentioned earlier in this chapter, buyers, like all other people, are subject to prejudices.

Many salesmen will have had the experience of presenting a rational argument to a buyer and getting his agreement only to find that his reason for buying is an emotional one such as his liking for the salesman's personality. Nevertheless, the rational approach is an important part of the analytical process and should be considered for each of the main buying interests.

Performance

The way the product or material functions is its true performance. In the case of a retailer who stocks branded goods for sale to the public the performance would be the rate of sale or stock turn of the product. The salesman can identify the buyer's interest if, when presenting his product, the buyer expresses a keen interest in such things as speed of operation, handling, quality of finish, standards of quality and, in the case of retailers, the rate of stock turn. Another aspect of performance is the after sales service. In the case of goods, such as motor-cars, typewriters and domestic appliances which require regular servicing, this can be considered as part of the performance of the product. A buyer who is interested in the performance of the product will show a keen interest in details of the servicing. He will, probably, want to know how frequently the product will require to be serviced, how much it will cost and if the supplier's servicing arrangements are adequate.

Once the salesman has identified performance as a main buying interest he should be prepared to supply the information to satisfy the interest.

Economy

The economy of a product may be simply the price but this would be an unusual instance. Economy is really value for money. It is often said that 'good things really cost less' because they outlast cheaper products and are, therefore, more economical in the long term. Sometimes the economy motive may be profit on the resale and it is worth remembering that a distributor's true profit is the net profit on each article multiplied by the number of articles sold.

Sometimes there is an appeal to economy if the product has an auxiliary use or a high re-sale value or scrap value. Most buyers express an interest in economy during their conversations with salesmen and the salesman should always try to identify which particular aspect of the economy motive is likely to be the main interest. A good way of presenting arguments to illustrate the economic advantages of a product is by taking pencil and paper and working out the economy points in front of the buyer so that he sees the calculations.

Durability

The lasting qualities of a product can be the major interest of some buyers. In some situations the cost of changing products can be considerable; machines may have to be stopped and dismantled. A product which lasts has a low rate of depreciation and, if it is used regularly, the user grows familiar with it and becomes more efficient with practice. With durability one associates reliability and confidence, both of which are qualities that a buyer comes to depend upon. Records of durability from other users, provided the necessary permission is given, can be quoted to substantiate effectively the claims which a salesman makes.

Appearance

The appearance of a product may be its main appeal, particularly if the design or colour features are an intrinsic part of the article. Fashion goods appeal mainly by their appearance but an up-to-date design of a traditional piece of equipment may have an equally strong appeal. This has been shown by the minor alterations in the design of ordinary tools by the incorporation of a grip handle.

The appeal of appearances is largely an emotional one and the salesman should tactfully ascertain the buyer's taste before enlarging too freely on this buying interest.

Safety

The appeal of safety can be a very strong one. Security and protection of the family and business interests loom very large in the minds of most people. If the product or service has particular safety features it may be possible to relate them to the buyer's needs and to illustrate how a particular incident may have been prevented or minimized.

The safety features should be isolated, the particular dangers which each is designed to avoid or minimize should be described and the principle by which the safety feature circumvents the danger should be explained.

The consequences of the danger can form a strong and dramatic appeal because so often a salesman is-able to quote reports from the popular press.

Comfort

Comfort is a friendly kind of appeal and most people are appreciative of it. The buyer to whom this appeal is important should be encouraged, if possible, to experience the comfort himself. If he is buying on behalf of someone else it may be possible to get the user to try the article and experience the benefits himself.

Where comfort is a main buying interest the demonstration becomes a most important part of the interview.

Adaptability

Some products are versatile and adaptable and their main appeal is because of this feature. It is closely allied to performance and economy. The demonstration again plays an important part and the buyer and user should be encouraged to use the product and see for themselves the wide range of uses to which it can be applied. The full range of uses should be explained and demonstrated thoroughly and the economies in both time and money pointed out so that the real advantages and benefits are clearly understood.

Publicity support

This interest is not often a main buying interest; usually it is subsidiary to some other interest and has a supporting appeal. When a buyer is likely to be impressed by the publicity support which the product receives the salesman should explain it thoroughly. The explanation should cover the policy behind the appeal of the publicity, the method chosen of making the appeal, the media chosen to publicize it and the benefits which the buyer can expect to receive as a result of the publicity campaign.

Distribution and service

The buyers of some products need a good delivery service and where this interest becomes a main buying issue the salesman should describe the service which his company has to offer. The number and location of depots, the range of stocks held in the depots, the times of opening and closing and the expected time taken to make deliveries are points which should be explained to the buyer.

Emotional Interests

Motivation Research is largely concerned with the emotional stimuli to buying. The main buying interests defined previously were concerned mostly with tangible advantages and benefits which could be demonstrated or proved to a buyer and were capable of description in absolute terms. Admittedly, comfort is emotional, but a buyer will notice the difference between a wooden chair and an upholstered armchair if he tries them both.

The emotional interests which stimulate a buyer cannot be defined in precise terms yet they are often strongly-held convictions which, sometimes, are maintained in the face of factual data to the contrary.

The analysis is difficult to make because emotional feelings are very complex. The salesman should not attempt to make a deep study of emotional impulses and should content himself with recognizing the main signs and appealing only to the emotions in a broad general way.

Attempts to analyse emotional behaviour too deeply will probably cause the buyer to raise a barrier against what he considers to be an intrusion into his personal feelings. Moreover, many buyers who buy because of emotional reasons are often genuinely unaware of them.

One of the difficulties which salesmen sometimes encounter is the strong desire from a buyer to purchase a product because of emotional reasons which are held back by a sense of guilt. A typical example is that of businessmen who wish to have luxuriously-furnished offices, modern equipment, expensive cars or some other status symbol which will proclaim their success. Often the desire to have these items is there but a rational admission that the luxury item is not strictly necessary holds the buyers' desires in check. The salesman is faced with the problem of rationalizing the desires of the businessman so that the purchase is seen to be a logical one justified by the advantages and benefits which it will bring.

There are some strong emotional instincts which the salesman should be able to recognize and these are discussed below.

Love

This is probably the most powerful of emotions and probably accounts for a large percentage of the sales of gifts. Toys and goods for children's hobbies will also be bought largely on the basis of affection. To the salesman selling commercially this emotion will not often be an important one but goods which may benefit the welfare of staff could come into the category where an emotional appeal is used. Effective selling sentences which may be used are:

'The installation of our strip lighting will not only improve the working conditions but will also raise the morale of your staff'. The proprietor of the business may then see himself as a benefactor.

'One of the benefits which our customers get when they install our noiseless electric typewriters is the feeling by the staff that their interests are looked after.'

Fear

The sales of many products such as locks, fire extinguishers, safety belts in cars are influenced by fear of loss or harm. The salesman does not need to paint an alarming picture of the disasters which may happen if a product is not purchased because there is such a general awareness of accidents. Every day newspapers carry details of some accident which might have been averted if only the victim had protected himself by buying some safety device.

Sentences which are pertinent to this emotion are:

'Insurance may reimburse you for the loss, due to fire, of material articles, but think of the inconvenience which would be caused if your business files were burnt. Our fireproof cabinet will preserve the contents in case of fire.'

'Each machine has a safety guard which is connected to a special switch in the motor. The machine will not start until the guard is in place and if the guard is moved the motor cuts out automatically.'

Pleasure

The contemplation of pleasure and enjoyment of it is one of the activities that makes life interesting and happy. Any product that can evoke the feeling of pleasure usually has an immediate appeal. The salesman has to be wary of a feeling of guilt of self-indulgence holding the buyer in check. As mentioned earlier, this may be a case of rationalizing the desires of the buyer in terms of advantages and benefits. This emotion can often be aroused by persuading the buyer to try the product and experience the pleasure himself. A personal trial will always be a more effective argument than a verbal recommendation.

Artistic appreciation

Many buyers who respond to the rational reasons for buying products can be influenced strongly by the aesthetic pleasure which is derived from good design. The design which is functional and elegant has an immense advantage over those products which are only functional. Many markets have been revolutionized by the introduction of new designs; Scandinavian furniture design is a notable example. There is a growing awareness among manufacturers that many functional products can be improved by better design. In some markets those manufacturers who have not realized the importance of design have suffered a severe setback. Even an ordinary tool like a hammer has been made more attractive by the re-design of the head and the incorporation of a shaped grip on the handle.

The salesman has an opportunity of complimenting the buyer's taste by remarks such as 'You are always ahead of your competitors in fashion and design so I'm sure you will want to see the new designs which we have just introduced.'

Pride

Pride is an emotion that is present in most people. It may be the pride of self-esteem; of achievement; of status and even of self-importance. Flattery often appeals very strongly to proud people. Flattery should be used with great care because when it is used overtly the buyer may become suspicious of the motives of the salesman. Most people like to feel important and like to be appreciated; the judicious use of compliments and the close attention paid to proud people enhances their self-appreciation. Most salesmen realize the value of using phrases such as:

'As you know the technical advantages of this machine, etc, etc.'

'With your experience in the industry you will appreciate the advantages that this product will bring in shortening the processing time.'

Sex

The sexual emotion plays a considerable part in the sale of cosmetics and toiletries and the desire of either sex to attract the other is a basic emotion. Any product that is likely to attract the owner to the opposite sex will have an instant basic appeal to most people. Fashion goods for both sexes come into this category and it is interesting to observe how much more fashion-conscious men have become during the last few years. Sales of modish men's clothes have increased and a much larger proportion of men now buy toiletries.

The salesman selling products which have a sexual appeal will probably agree that it is indelicate to make a direct reference to the attraction. The indirect reference is likely to be more effective and phrases such as the following may be useful:

'These are the new styles which have become so popular on the Riviera.'

'Lancelot Just, the film star, wears a jacket like this.'

Association

This emotional appeal has been described as the 'herd instinct' and is the strong urge of people to belong to a group. There are usually overtones of emulation about the appeal which are related to improvements or ambition. Young girls copy the styles of film stars and business men buy the clothes and equipment which they associate with successful men. The desire can be aroused in a similar way as the example of the appeal given above for a jacket.

If the salesman wishes to quote an example of the product in use elsewhere he should take care that the individual or company using the product is one which the buyer holds in esteem.

Curiosity

Unusual products sometimes sell as a consequence of the curiosity of buyers. Many shops which sell foreign foods do so to a number of buyers who merely wish to try for themselves. The use of curiosity as an appeal is usually a good way to secure a buyer's attention and can often be combined with novelty. Curiosity can be a sign of intelligence and a buyer with a curious mind should have his curiosity assuaged with as much information as possible.

It is not easy to close a sale with curiosity as the main motive but many sales have been made as a result of the initial curiosity of the buyer.

Health

Many products have a health appeal. Some foods, proprietary medicines, sports equipment and some types of holidays all appeal to some extent to the desire for health of the buyers. The salesman should be careful not to dwell heavily on the consequences of deprivation but should concentrate more on the positive advantages of enjoying good health.

Creative urge

The growth of Do-It-Yourself activities is evidence of the importance of the creative urge. In the food trade it was quickly discovered that some 'Instant' products, to which only water had to be added, lacked appeal to the housewife. She wanted to indulge her desire to create and when this was realized the product was changed and the housewife had to add some ingredients and mix. The sales recovered and the product became an established one.

If the salesman's product is likely to appeal to the creative urge he should try to get the buyer to use a sample or take some part in the creation if it is possible.

Although the main buying interests and the emotional interests have been treated separately the salesman will know from experience that they are often not separate in the buyer's mind. He will often have to leaven a rational sales argument with an appeal to an emotional interest and sales often result from a judicious admixture.

Psychological Adjustments by the Salesman

The importance of the salesman being able to judge how other people react to his personality has been mentioned before. It is virtually impossible for a salesman to read the mind of each buyer and to know exactly what effect his personality is having on him. But the salesman must make a 'judgment'. What is also important is that he must make his judgment quickly and act upon it.

When the judgment has been made the salesman often has to make a psychological adjustment. An example which illustrates this is when, say, an irate customer makes an allegation about the salesman's company which is a very serious charge of deception but which is completely untrue. The first reaction which most salesmen will have is one of irritation and perhaps anger; this reaction will probably be stifled by the salesman's natural self-control and most salesmen will give 'the soft answer that turneth away wrath'. How many salesmen will adjust themselves quickly to see the good points which can be made of a slanderous attack?

It is in situations like these that the salesman must learn to pick out the good points and learn to adjust himself quickly. In the example quoted above the anger of the customer might be turned to advantage, if, say, the salesman says quietly:

'That was a very serious allegation which you made and I can understand your anger. I should react the same way myself if it were true. I'm glad you raised this point because we prefer to deal with customers who are straightforward like ourselves and who do not practise deception. The story which you have told is not true and this is why.' And the salesman carries on with his explanation.

Psychological adjustment by the salesman is very much a matter of intelligence and self-control. Before a man can influence others he needs to know himself thoroughly and to be in complete control of himself. With intelligence and self-control a salesman should use self analysis.

Self analysis can be practised easily and successfully every day. After each sales interview the salesman should examine it critically and ask himself:

'Was it a good interview?'
'Could it have been better?'
'How could I have improved it?'
'What went wrong?'

Such self analysis is not morbid introspection but helps a salesman to identify and learn from his mistakes so that he can avoid them in the future. By consciously carrying out this simple mental discipline the salesman schools himself to make mental adjustments to meet the different situations which can arise.

There are two main kinds of mental adjustment which the salesman should try to make. These are adjustments in his mental attitude as a reaction to the buyer and the adjustment of his mental attitude to his own shortcomings.

As far as reaction to the buyer is concerned the salesman should always seek the positive advantages in a situation. The best way of doing this is to align oneself with the buyer's mood and then lead him on to some positive point.

Examples of the way this can be done are:

A surly buyer may be provided with an excuse for his surliness by some such remark as, 'Yours must be an exacting job – having to examine the merits of different products and listen to the claims and sales talk of so many salesmen. I doubt if I could be as even tempered as you always manage to be'. This remark is perhaps too flattering but if it were a little less obvious the buyer would probably feel pleased that he was considered to be even-tempered. Most surly people are half ashamed of their attitude and would like an excuse to abandon it.

The buyer who is arrogant and dictatorial may be mollified by the salesman who reacts and says, 'It's always a pleasure to come to see you because, unlike so many of the people I see, you know the products well and you make up your mind.'

Sometimes remarks like these may rebound to the salesman's disadvantage but only experience will teach him how to react and adjust himself to different buyers. The important thing which the salesman should know is that he should learn to react and treat buyers in a manner which is suitable to their various personalities. The salesman should look at his buyers and consider each as an individual. He should reflect and decide what kind of personality traits each one possesses. It is a very short step, when the salesman has made his analysis, for him to decide on an individual way of handling his different buyers. If the salesman is consciously aware of the need for an individual approach to each buyer he will very quickly develop the talent and ability for it.

The other psychological adjustment which the salesman should try to make is more difficult. It is sometimes said that 'we never see ourselves as others see us'. If this were true it would be impossible to see our own personality faults. Fortunately most people are aware of some of their faults and can take steps to cure them. The difficulties arise when the faults have become habits and are continued unconsciously.

When an individual makes an unusual error in personal behaviour he often realizes that he has made a mistake. The realization may be immediate and he may be able to correct his error; on the other hand he may realize the error too late to make a correction. If realization comes, he can at least try to avoid making the mistake again.

The use of a tape recorder was mentioned in Chapter 1 as a helpful aid for the salesman when judging the impression which he makes on others. A tape recording of his voice can also help the salesman to understand the reactions of buyers to his personality. It is important, however, when considering the voice and its effect on others to guard against affectation. A natural voice has an honest and sincere ring about it which is pleasing to listeners.

The kind of faults which are common among people and which many have without being conscious of them are:

Egotism

Many people are too fond of saying 'I' and 'my'. They are prone to interrupt others and to dominate the conversation. Their experiences and their opinions are, in their view, important. The salesman should guard against this fault and, whenever the temptation arises for him to interrupt or recount an irrelevant experience, he should pause and let someone else do the talking. Many people acquire a reputation for sagacity by keeping silent. If the salesman is on the look-out for this fault he will quickly become aware of it.

Disparagement

Disparaging competitors' products is a common fault, yet it is one of the surest ways of destroying the buyers' confidence in the salesman who disparages and in his products. Sometimes the habit even spreads to disparagement, by inference, of the buyer and his judgment. Remarks such as 'You need a new machine for this kind of work because, as everyone knows, the model you have was never any good,' are a direct insult to the buyer if he bought the machine.

The salesman should always remember the advice that 'if you can't say anything good about it, say nothing'. It is not suggested that a salesman should pointedly praise his competitors; after all, there is another saying, 'charity begins at home'.

Boastfulness

Fortunately, not many people are guilty of continual boasting. Most people boast on occasions over some achievement of which they are specially proud and, provided they don't repeat it too often, their friends regard it with tolerance as a human foible. Boasting to a customer comes into a different category because it may refer to the product and be, in effect, an extravagant claim. This can be a serious misdemeanour of selling and is tantamount to misleading the buyer. It should always be avoided.

Superiority

The salesman or anyone who 'knows it all' is a bore to almost everyone. It is bad enough to be classed as a bore but human nature being what it is, people positively delight in catching out the 'know all'. The salesman who lays down the law in uncompromising terms really lays down a challenge and positively incites buyers to catch him out and they usually do.

Verbosity

It is a long time since salesmen were described as 'having the gift of the gab'. But there are still some salesmen who insist on doing all the talking. With remarkable diligence they tell every buyer all the selling points and are often surprised at the few orders which result. Salesmen who are even only a little guilty of this fault should remember that the buyer may also have an opinion and want to express it; and if he is not allowed to talk he will not be able to give the order. Listening is just as important as talking, often more so.

No salesman is perfect but those who are willing to concede that they may have faults and wish to find them and try to correct them will have no difficulty in making the necessary psychological adjustments. The right attitude of mind is the greatest asset which a salesman can have when making adjustments of this nature.

The Most Important Psychological Points

In considering psychological attitudes, the salesman should never adopt an artificial attitude. He should behave in his natural manner but should always temper his attitudes and his remarks with an understanding and consideration for the attitudes, behaviour and points of view of his customers.

The salesman who genuinely tries to understand his customers without sacrificing his own convictions begins to build a positive relationship which can form the basis of mutual trust and respect.

The competent salesman often achieves more by listening than by talking. Listening inspires confidence and helps create understanding. It is also a technique which can be used effectively when overcoming objections and handling complaints.

6 Overcoming Objections and Handling Complaints

Objections are, in many situations, an integral part of the sales interview and should always be regarded as a positive and not as a negative step towards completing the sale.

Few achievements are gained without difficulties, and objections during a sales interview can act as stimuli to the salesman. It is not suggested that the difficulties which a salesman meets will act as a kind of adrenalin or stimulating drug but that objections can be used to help him.

When a buyer starts to raise a few objections which are genuine it is a sure sign that he is really interested in the product. The objections are a demand to be convinced that the product is all that the salesman claims for it. A salesman should always welcome objections as evidence that the buyer is taking his offer seriously. Most salesmen will agree that the most difficult buyers are probably those who are uncommunicative. If only these buyers could be persuaded to raise a few objections the salesmen would have some idea of how to proceed. Similarly, it is very difficult to handle buyers who accept and agree to all the sales arguments which are put forward but yet refuse to buy.

The positive step which objections can take towards closing the sale is that they can provide the salesman with an insight into the buyer's attitude towards the offer which has been made. Objections are signposts and guides which the salesman can use. The salesman should use them as a sales aid and should never attempt to stifle them.

As each sales point is put to the buyer the salesman should always check that the point has been understood and the advantage or benefit is accepted. The salesman need only ask a few courteous questions such as:

'Is this the kind of performance that you want?'
'Does this match up to your expectations?'

Questions like these may bring agreement, in which case the salesman can proceed to his next sales point. If the question brings an objection, the salesman has an opportunity of dealing with it and satisfying the buyer. After dealing with the objection the salesman should always check again by asking:

'Does that cover the point which you raised?' or
'Is that satisfactory?'

A frank enquiry will usually bring a frank response and the opportunity to go over some doubtful point afresh.

The regular checking of sales points throughout the interview helps the salesman by recording steps towards the buyer's satisfaction. The provocation which these checks may have in bringing out objections is an integral part of satisfying the buyer's needs and the salesman should accept them as stepping stones to the order.

There are various tactful ways of handling objections when they first arise and the salesman should cultivate them and use them regularly. Examples are:

'That means you are interested in . . . so I'll explain that more fully.'

'I'm pleased you've raised that point because it's an interesting part of the product and I'd like to tell you more about it.'

By using such sentences the salesman avoids the overt flattery contained in such obvious remarks as:

'That's a most interesting question. I see you know all about this product.'

At no time should the salesman refer to objections; he should always refer to the question, the point or the comment.

If the salesman treats all objections as requests for further and fuller information he will quickly cultivate an easy, confident manner in handling them.

Occasionally a buyer will raise objections in a hostile manner and the salesman should always be careful to avoid falling into the trap of becoming involved in an argument. It is easy to win an argument and lose an order and sometimes lose a buyer for good.

There are some objections which salesmen create themselves and these can be avoided if the salesman reflects on his own attitude towards buyers and sometimes his personal attitude towards other people.

Avoiding the Creation of Objections

Unwittingly many salesmen create hostility and objections by their own behaviour. They do this by not cultivating the right selling habits. Bad selling habits create objections and may well be called selling misdemeanours. Some of the more common faults of salesmen are listed below.

Muddle

This can arise from untidiness and lack of preparation. It may arise because the salesman has not taken the trouble to sort out his leaflets, his samples or demonstration kit. When he wants to show the buyer some article he has to turn out his case and conduct a search. The same characteristic is shown if an illogical or ill-balanced sales argument is put to the buyer. If the salesman is demonstrating a product and he shows the start of the operation and then the end and finally the middle part of the operation he will confuse and bewilder the buyer. A muddled salesman gives the impression that he represents a muddled company and is selling a muddled product.

Exaggeration

The too-frequent use of superlatives and exaggerated claims can arouse hostility very easily. Most people have an instinctive and hostile reaction to this behaviour. It is almost as though the buyer has been challenged to contradict the salesman and dared to deny some claim. It is a great temptation when faced with such a situation to try to knock the salesman off his perch or prick the bubble of over confidence. This is such a common reaction that it finds expression in stock comic situations when the clown persuades the ringmaster to sit on his own top hat. The delight of the audience in the deflation of pomposity is sufficient evidence of the dangers of making exaggerated claims.

Disparagement

Very frequently a salesman can, unwittingly, disparage the buyer. Chance remarks about the performance of old equipment, the unfashionable goods in stock or the need for modern up-to-date merchandise can reflect a criticism of the buyer's past judgment. Open disparagement of buyers is a very rare offence among salesmen because it is too obvious a mistake to make. It is the minor, unconscious habits or remarks which can arouse hostility. Failure to take an interest in what a buyer is saying is a common fault. The salesman, too often, is over eager to put his point of view and, when the buyer has finished talking, he sometimes, rapidly, puts forward a sales argument and ignores the previous comments of the buyer.

The buyer's judgment can easily be disparaged unintentionally by too blatant a comparison between the product being offered and the products normally stocked. Similarly, when a salesman feels it necessary to air his knowledge in order to impress a buyer, he often only succeeds in presenting himself as a 'know all'. The habit of talking down to a buyer can be a source of strong irritation, particularly as some buyers are very knowledgeable and often know more about their products than the salesmen. The salesmen should scrupulously avoid any hint of disparagement.

Overtalking

Most salesmen have confessed that, on some occasions, they have talked themselves into an order and then talked themselves out of it. This is a great danger among keen and over enthusiastic salesmen who often forget that the buyer may have a point of view and want to express it. The sales presentation is not a lecture at which the buyer is a pupil but should be a conversation between two people in which the buyer takes part. The buyer should be encouraged to express his opinions and voice any objections which he may have. If the salesman encourages the buyer to talk and he is an attentive, interested listener he will probably learn more about the buyer's needs and problems than if he talks himself. Overtalking will often merely keep objections under the surface and partially stifle them. The buyer quickly becomes aware that the salesman is not really interested in dealing with his personal needs or satisfying his demands. One of the salesman's objectives should be to bring the buyer's objections out into the open so that he can answer them satisfactorily.

Appearance

The initial impression which a salesman makes is of considerable importance and he should always present himself in the best possible manner. An untidy, ill-kempt salesman reflects discredit on the company which employs him. A salesman who is clean and wears neat, tidy well-brushed clothes starts with an advantage.

Discourtesy

Few salesmen are openly rude to buyers but, as with disparagement minor discourtesies can be committed unwittingly. Some buyers resent salesmen taking things for granted such as hanging up their coats and hats or seating themselves without an invitation. A common fault is that of smoking uninvited or clearing a space on the buyer's desk or counter without asking permission to do so. It is always advisable to seek permission in a courteous way for any of the small personal actions which a salesman may wish to do.

All the selling misdemeanours mentioned above imply directly or indirectly a lack of consideration on the part of the salesman for the buyer's status. They imply a disregard for the niceties of social behaviour and a diminution of the buyer's position. The salesman in committing them creates an impression that it was not worth his while to make even a modest effort to impress the buyer favourably. It is not suggested that the salesmen should be servile but merely that they should politely observe the normal courtesies of social intercourse.

Preventing Objections Arising

There are often opportunities which a salesman can use to prevent objections being raised at all. This is not meant as a technique to stifle them and thus leave the buyer unsatisfied but as a way of answering them before they arise.

In his day-to-day experience of selling, the salesman should note the frequency with which objections are raised. Some objections will occur quite often and others on rare occasions. By making a mental note the salesman can list the more common objections and can work out ways and means of overcoming them. It is better, however, if he can forestall them by including his answers in his original sales presentation. If, for example, he knows that most customers ask how long the product will wear and are doubtful about its wearing qualities, he can incorporate this information early in his presentation.

This method of preventing objections is a useful one because it demonstrates to the buyer that the salesman understands the practical working of the product. The same kind of technique can be used when selling consumer expendables. Very often a dealer may be doubtful of the quantity that he can sell or how he should sell the product. The salesman can forestall this objection by suggesting a certain quantity and mentioning that the best results may be achieved by association with other products. The sales of mustard are likely to increase if the mustard is displayed next to bacon or cooked meats. Tins of fruit and tins of cream are a natural association.

When a salesman uses this method of forestalling an objection he can often consolidate his point by asking if the situation which has been covered is one that is likely to arise and whether the explanation covers the buyer's particular needs. In following this procedure the salesman not only forestalls the objection but satisfies it before it can arise.

This technique can be used to forestall most common objections whether they are technical or deal with the service or with price. Many salesmen anticipate price objections by presenting the quality, performance, service or saleability of their goods convincingly and, when the price is mentioned, it appears low in comparison to the value which has been established in the buyer's mind. By talking of quality and performance the salesman begins to build an image in the buyer's mind that the product is valuable. If the product is a machine the salesman may be able to talk of savings which the performance will bring. It is a common argument to quote savings and relate them to the cost of the product and then work out how long it will be before the cost is recovered by the savings. Such a phrase as 'This machine will have paid for itself in eighteen months from the savings which it will make' illustrates the way that this can be done.

By following a sales presentation which will build quality or performance the salesman is preparing his buyer for the price and may prevent an objection from arising. Salesmen should remember the saying 'It is not price which is too high but quality which is too low'.

The ability to sell the quality of a product is a mark of good salesmanship and selling the quality is a sound way of preventing objections arising. Many salesmen baulk at the idea of quality as a means of meeting objections but it should be considered more deeply.

The desire for quality is a universal characteristic. A very short reflection will convince most people of the validity of this statement. Most people, as children, wanted better sports equipment such as tennis rackets or cricket bats similar to those used by famous players. As adults, people prefer to own better tools and equipment and are always proud in their possession of good quality articles.

The instinct to strive for something better and to possess better quality goods is a fundamental one in mankind. This instinct is probably one of the mainsprings of the continuing development of civilization. It is latent in all people and the salesman should try to arouse and develop it.

The appeal of quality is deep-seated and the salesman who stresses this aspect of his goods can only do so if he has confidence in them and can, therefore, speak with conviction. The salesman's confidence in the quality of the goods communicates itself readily to the buyer and relieves him of anxieties. A buyer who has bought quality does not have worries about complaints, failures to meet specifications and grumbles from the staff in his company who will have to use the product. Many buyers are willing to pay extra for the added advantages which quality buying will bring.

Techniques of Handling Objections

Objections can be considered one of the mainstays of a salesman's existence. If none was raised the need for salesmen would be diminished. The salesman's job is largely a matter of handling and overcoming objections and he should welcome them as positive evidence of the buyer's interest. The buyer who raises no objections and does not buy has obviously not had his interest aroused. Objections give the salesman an opportunity to get to grips with the buyer's real needs. It is important, however, to recognize when the objection is a real one or merely a device to get rid of the salesman. If the salesman suspects that the objection is not genuine he should try, by tactful questions, to find the real obstacle in the buyer's mind.

When a buyer discloses an objection the salesman should immediately give it serious consideration. It may seem obvious to say that he should listen attentively and, if necessary, question the buyer about the objection. Careful attention and questioning regarding an objection has five positive advantages.

1 The objection often diminishes as the buyer is encouraged to talk about it.
2 The salesman, by questioning, tactfully learns full details of the objection. If it is not genuine he may be able, at this stage, to find the real objection.
3 He flatters the buyer by the serious attention that he gives to the problem.

4 He gains the time in which to formulate his answers.

5 By questioning he may also change the objection into a question which both the buyers and salesman join in providing an answer.

The salesman should, by following the technique of careful listening and questioning, try to find the basis of the objection. It may be price, quality, service, performance or some other feature which, in the buyer's view, is lacking.

Whatever the objection the salesman should be able to draw on his experience and knowledge to provide a convincing answer. A convincing answer can be improved if the facts are substantiated by an independent authority. Such an authority may be another customer who is willing to allow his name to be used for recommendations, it may be an independent report published by a trade or technical paper or consumer association or it may be a market research report. In such cases it is often an advantage to build up the independence and qualifications of the independent authority in the same way as counsel will qualify witnesses at a court case.

Sometimes objections are raised in a disparaging and personal way. When this happens the salesman should on no account allow himself to get flustered or heated but should remain calm and in full control of himself and of the sales interview.

It is sometimes a help, when objections arise, to use a little flattery such as, 'I see, Mr Smith, you understand the practical use of this product and I'm glad you've raised that point'. At other times the repetition of the objection by the salesman, will confirm that the salesman has grasped the point of the objection and intends to deal with it seriously. Both of these techniques can lead naturally to the demonstration or re-demonstration to cover the particular point.

When the objection has been answered satisfactorily, the salesman should always ask the buyer frankly if he is satisfied with the answer and, if the buyer is satisfied, he should continue with his sales presentation.

Typical Objections

There are a number of typical objections which often arise and, while the methods of handling them will vary from trade to trade, there are some general principles which can be applied or adopted.

The dismissal

This happens to almost every salesman and comes in a variety of ways. The buyer may say he has another appointment, that he is too busy or may suggest that the salesman should come back later. There are an infinite number of ways by which a buyer can intimate that he is not really interested in the salesman or his goods and wants to cut the interview short.

The best way to answer this objection is for the salesman to offer to make an appointment for another time but to include with his request a statement of the amount of time he will require. He may, for example, say, 'I'm very sorry to have arrived at an inopportune time. May I make an appointment for this afternoon (or some other suitable time)? I'd like to discuss our product for only twenty minutes'. Faced with the alternatives of making an appointment or granting an immediate interview most buyers usually respond by granting an immediate interview with the proviso that it can only last, say, ten minutes. The dismissal is often a false objection and conceals the buyer's lack of interest. If the buyer says there is really no point in making arrangements for another interview the salesman can express surprise and mention the leading advantages of his product which should claim the buyer's attention.

Overstocked

There are few salesmen who have not, at some time, been told by a buyer that he already has too much stock. This may be a genuine objection which the salesman has to accept. In such circumstances he should concentrate on persuading the buyer to dispose of the stock more quickly. Suggestions for wider uses of the product may be helpful. Other suggestions could relate to the display in association with other products or the siting of the stock in another and busier part of the shop if the objection comes from a retailer.

If the customer is a wholesaler the salesman may suggest useful selling ideas which the wholesaler's salesmen can use. The mention of suitable selling points may be helpful. On occasions the wholesaler may ask the manufacturer's salesman to talk to his own sales staff and give them sales ideas direct.

When the salesman suspects that the buyer is making an excuse or is perhaps overstocked with competitive goods he should stress the advantages of his own product and should point out the things which the buyer is missing by not using or selling the salesman's product.

No demand

Buyers often consider this reason to be a complete answer to a salesman's presentation. It can be answered easily by the suggestion that customers only ask for a product which they know is in stock. If this comment is followed up by the salesman's genuine claims that the product is stocked and sold in the district by his customer's competitors it will be a convincing answer. This objection is most common among wholesale and retail distributors and when it applies to a new product it is obviously a genuine claim.

With new products the salesman can point out the advantages over existing products. He may be able to show details of advance publicity and the promotional plans for the future. There are considerable advantages to be gained by distributors, who take a new product into stock when it first comes on to the market, if it turns out to be a success. The prospects of success should be explained to distributors but obviously care should be taken to avoid over-exaggeration.

Lack of authority

Lack of authority to buy is sometimes real and the decision has to be referred to a more senior executive. One of the best ways to handle this kind of objection is to assume that the individual who cannot buy is the one who has the authority. By deferring to his judgment and taking great pains to convince the man who may be the under-buyer, the salesman may obtain an influential supporter.

If the under-buyer is treated as though he has the knowledge, experience and competence to buy but lacks the authority, he is more likely to help the salesman. When the disclosure is made that the sanction of higher authority is needed the salesman should courteously but frankly ask the under-buyer if he may have his permission to seek an interview with the real buyer. An open request often avoids the embarrassment which can be felt by the under-buyer at having to reveal his lack of authority.

False authority

Occasionally a salesman will encounter an executive who gives the impression that he has the authority to buy but becomes evasive when a decision has to be made. This can be an awkward situation because there may be considerable loss of face by the executive when the true situation comes to light. The salesman should seek a tactful way out by assuming, as in the case of the under-buyer who hasn't the authority but is straightforward and admits the situation, that the executive has the knowledge, experience and competence but due to management reasons has not yet been given the authority.

No need

This may often be a genuine objection because no salesman can really be sure that his products fill the buyer's needs until he has established the needs. When faced with this situation the salesman can say with a wry smile that he is genuinely sorry to hear this but could he explain very briefly what he has to offer just in case there is some point which may have been overlooked. Most buyers will respond to a candid approach and be prepared to allow some time to the salesman who is frank and courteous.

Satisfied with present suppliers

Customers who give this objection as a reason for not buying are worth more than average attention. Customer loyalty to suppliers is what most salesmen are trying to create and every salesman seeks to build a circle of loyal customers. When a salesman succeeds in winning business from a customer who shows loyalty to his suppliers he has gained, as a rule, more than an initial order. Faced with this objection the salesman can congratulate the buyer and say how pleased he is to hear it. The salesman can go on to say that customer loyalty is a very good thing and he is very pleased to say that he has a large number of loyal customers.

The advantages of loyalty should be mentioned and agreed but not overstressed. The line of approach which may be used with advantage is, 'An enterprising business is always willing to examine new products and new sources of supply as otherwise it cannot progress,' or 'We don't want to persuade you to change from one supplier to another but merely wish to point out the advantages and benefits which our products can offer'.

Poor reputation

Occasionally a salesman is met with a challenging statement that his company has a poor reputation. The statement may be based on previous experience of the buyer or on hearsay evidence. If the belief is held because of previous experience, the salesman should treat the objection almost as a complaint and should investigate the details and try to right the situation. Hearsay evidence is difficult to combat because usually there is a reluctance to disclose the source and details. In such cases the salesman should try to obtain as much of the evidence or basis for the belief as possible. Having got some of the background it should be possible to refute the allegations in part by quoting the number of satisfied customers or specific performance details which have been achieved and relate to the problem. It is always useful if a salesman can persuade a nucleus of his customers to give personal recommendations; these are best handled personally on the basis that a new prospect be allowed to telephone and talk to the satisfied customer direct. Testimonials and written recommendations are sometimes suspect and, particularly when the same ones are in continuous use, the impression may be given that they refer to the distant past.

Satisfied with present model

This objection usually applies to capital equipment such as cash registers, office machinery, plant in factories or any items such as consumer durables. The belief expressed is usually genuine and springs from continued satisfaction and a lack of knowledge of performance standards of new equipment. To handle this type of objection the salesman needs to know his product and its performance thoroughly. He also needs to know the competitive products and their performances and particularly the performance of the equipment in use. Having established the current performance level the salesman should make tactful comparisons, preferably making any calculations in front of the buyer. Estimated savings, higher output and the greater versatility of the more modern equipment can then be pointed out and as each subject is covered in turn a formidable list of advantages can be compiled.

Too dear

This objection was partially dealt with earlier in this chapter but the methods of dealing with it can vary considerably. If the objection can be forestalled by building up the quality or performance of the product, this is probably the best way. Quite often an objection on price, particularly with a keen buyer, comes early in the interview. Such a buyer may be trying to establish low price as a condition before discussing the product seriously. Remarks such as 'It's no use talking to me about anything if it costs more than . . . ' are the preliminary skirmishes of bargaining.

The experienced salesman is rarely unsettled by shock tactics and his knowledge and experience of the trade, buyers' techniques (they have them as well as salesmen) and competitors' prices will stand him in good stead on these occasions. Knowledge of current prices of competitors' goods is a considerable asset when price objections arise. The salesman cannot very well contradict a buyer if he doubts the accuracy of the figures quoted but if he has a shrewd idea of current prices he can gauge the strength of the objection. When a direct objection on price comes up the salesman may sometimes deal with it successfully by a forthright statement such as, 'I don't suppose price is the only factor when you buy. You have to be sure that, even if the price is low, the goods are satisfactory.' The salesman should utilize his knowledge of the main buying interests of each buyer and should seek to establish the satisfaction of these before getting involved in price negotiation.

Most buyers will readily agree, when pressed, that they do not buy on price alone and will be willing to discuss the other factors. This gives the salesman the chance to build up the quality, performance, service and, perhaps, trouble-free association which already exists. By the time price comes up again the salesman should have assessed by tactful questioning, an estimate of the difference in price.

No matter whether the difference is large or small the salesman should relate his advantages to the difference. This method can be illustrated by using a product with which all salesmen are familiar; a car.

A salesman faced with a car buyer, whether he is a private buyer or a fleet buyer, can usually isolate the differences in prices because the prices are generally known. Having established the difference he can say, 'For only another £x you will have larger tyres which are safer and more comfortable, heavier gauge metal on the bodywork which means higher second hand value and extra durability, figure contoured seating, etc., etc . . . '

Price can be made to look small by breaking it down to so much per day in use or so much per article, and the advantages made to seem more worthwhile in comparison. When competitors' prices are not generally known the salesman can still follow the same technique, but unless he is very knowledgeable about price levels, he is on less sure ground and should proceed more cautiously. Sometimes the price objection is really a matter of terms when, for example, a dealer claims he gets better terms from a competing manufacturer. It is a difficult objection to meet because authority for changing terms may be outside the salesman's province. The salesman has little choice but to maintain that terms are sanctioned by Head Office and that he can only seriously recommend that they be revised if the customer either buys the minimum quantity for better terms or changes from being, say, a retailer to becoming a wholesaler. The ways of dealing with demands for better terms depend very much on individual company policy but the salesman should continue to press home the other advantages which his products may have. Many products hold their position in the market in the face of unfavourable margins by virtue of the public demand and/or the quality of the product.

Not ready to buy just yet

There are many buyers who are hesitant and who procrastinate. All the essential ingredients of a successful sale may have been carried out but the buyer, whilst agreeing with the salesman, still wishes to postpone the decision. On most occasions it is an inability on the part of the buyer to make up his own mind. The salesman may have to sell and buy, that is he may have to make up the buyer's mind for him. This kind of objection is really best covered by a good technique of closing the sale. The salesman can point out all the advantages and benefits which the buyer is missing by not placing an order. By creating a sense of urgency and by using a positive closing technique the interview may often be brought to a successful conclusion.

Dealing with Complaints

Most salesmen have to handle complaints occasionally and these may be from traders or users. Some companies have a standard procedure and special complaint forms and the salesman has little difficulty in dealing with them.

The proper handling of complaints can change a situation from embarrassment to one of satisfaction and future goodwill. When a complaint arises the salesman has the chance to discuss a matter of personal concern to the complainant. Furthermore, it is usually a situation where he has the undivided attention and interest of the person concerned.

Complaints can sometimes lead to litigation and, for this reason, the salesman, as a responsible employee of his company, should never admit personal or company liability. It is important to follow this rule in all circumstances because even the most innocuous complaint may sometimes build up into a complex and serious matter. The frequent press reports of litigants seeking damages is a warning of how involved and costly some proceedings can become.

If the possibility of legal action by a complainant arises, no matter how remotely, the salesman should advise his sales manager or responsible executive so that the company can consider the policy issues involved. His initial role, in such a case, should be confined to the collection of information only and then acting under specific instructions from his company.

When a complaint arises the salesman's task is, first of all, to collect all the informaton which may be relevant. In the cases where the company policy allows a salesman to deal with complaints on the spot and to settle them with a replacement, he should, of course, do this promptly. As a general principle it is advantageous to settle complaints expeditiously and a straight, on the spot, replacement if authorized by the company, will save the time, trouble and expense of everyone concerned and probably gain goodwill.

Where a more complicated situation arises or the salesman is not authorized to settle on the spot he should assemble the following kind of information about the complaint:

1 *Nature of the complaint.*
   This should include the kind of complaint, for example, unusually quick wear, defective parts, misuse, breakages or poor operating performance. Complaints regarding packaging such as the inclusion of foreign bodies in packages would be noted under this heading.

2 *The circumstances or conditions under which the complaint arose.*
   The goods may have been faulty on arrival at the customer's premises, they may have been dropped or used under improper conditions, they may have been used by untrained personnel.

3 *The time and date of the complaint.*
   This may have some bearing on the method of dealing with it because sometimes date stamped products are used outside the warranty period and the manufacturer may quite rightly refuse to accept liability.

4 *The names and addresses of the people concerned or witnesses to the complaint.*

Details of witnesses names and addresses may be unnecessary and care should be taken not to offend a customer by taking details of the private address of an employee. The value and importance of this information depends very much on the nature of the complaint but sometimes it is essential.

5 *The goods under complaint.*

If the complaint concerns an article which is in a fit state to be removed and some advantage may be obtained by sending it back to Head Office for a thorough examination the salesman should do so. The article, however, is probably the customer's property and his permission will be necessary. If the complaint concerns a batch, then the salesman should try to obtain a representative sample for examination.

6 *Details of any damage, loss or injury suffered.*

The salesman should exercise considerable tact and should never give the impression of seeking this kind of information. If details are offered he should accept them and record them accurately but should not provoke them.

7 *The name and address of the supplier of the goods if supplied other than direct from the factory.*

The possibility of damage in transit or storage on a distributor's premises should be considered and, if a carrier has been used, his name and address should be obtained.

8 *The date on which the goods were supplied, manufacture date and batch number if any.*

This information may be of value if a batch control system is in operation and may enable the salesman's company to examine manufacturing records which were compiled at the same time of manufacture as the goods under complaint.

9 *Particulars of other goods used in association.*

If the product is blended, mixed or used in conjunction with any other product the salesman should get as much detailed information as possible. It may be difficult to obtain samples and details but the attempt should be made.

10 *The storage conditions under which the goods have been kept.*

The keeping qualities may have been affected by variations in temperature and humidity and the product may have deteriorated.

11 *Any company information such as order numbers, invoice or delivery note numbers.*

This may help to check on the conditions under which the product reached the complainant.

All the above information may not be necessary but it is helpful when handling complaints to have as much knowledge as possible. Some companies have a definite credit policy for certain categories of complaint and allow the salesman freedom within certain limits to operate the policy and to grant a stipulated allowance.

Salesmen can demonstrate their ability to handle awkward situations if they are successful in containing complaints and settling them amicably on the spot. A complaint which is handled tactfully and fairly can result in increased goodwill and can establish the reputation of the salesman's company with an individual and probably with his immediate circle of friends.

Complaints afford an opportunity to create goodwill. Complainants always listen attentively when their complaints are discussed.

At such a time, with the complainant's keen attention, the salesman should recognize the occasion as an opportunity to impress his customer with the company's concern to deal with customers in a fair and efficient manner.

Points to Remember

The good salesman always avoids the careless behaviour, mentioned earlier in this chapter, which can create objections or a hostile attitude from the buyer. He also builds into his presentation the answers to some of the more common objections of which he has experience. But it is in the handling of objections that the salesman can really practise his skills. The basic tactics are for the salesman to listen carefully, to question politely in order to ascertain the requirements which will satisfy the buyer and then to present his case tactfully but with direct reference to the buyer's needs.

The same care and attention which the salesman uses to overcome objections should also be applied to the handling of complaints.

7 Sales Reporting and Records

Report writing is often regarded by salesmen as an irksome and unnecessary chore. Many salesmen stoutly declare that their job is to get orders and not to write reports. This view often arises from the suspicion that the reports which have been sent to Head Office have been accepted without comment or interest.

Management is often guilty of demanding regular reports at daily, weekly or monthly intervals in the belief that these reports act as a form of control. General reports of this nature where the salesman is given no specific objective rarely achieve the purpose of control. If they are received without comment, they are often written hurriedly and without interest. In such situations the salesman can scarcely be blamed for his hostile attitude to report writing.

To appreciate the value of reports the salesman should reflect on his role and function and remember that part of his function is to keep his management informed of all activities on his territory. The management of many companies is dependent upon the salesmen for market information and sometimes the salesmen are almost the sole source. This is a considerable responsibility and covers a wide field of investigation.

The salesman who realizes the importance of keeping his management fully and accurately informed is playing a valuable part in the management of the company when he sends in good reports. He not only informs his management of the facts and his opinions of the situation on his territory but he demonstrates that he is knowledgeable and alive to what is taking place.

A good report from a salesman may often have a wide circulation at Head Office. If it contains unusual information, backed by evidence, or well reasoned opinions, the report may be circulated among the directors and top managers. The salesman who is successful at selling and who writes good reports may, in developing his report-writing talent, be taking the first step towards management responsibilities. A report gives a salesman the opportunity of showing that he understands the requirements of management and can supply some of the necessary information for management decisions.

Some companies have printed report forms, with or without specific headings, and sometimes a report is required for each call which is made. Where such forms exist the salesman will obviously use them, but often there is a space for general remarks where there is scope for him to express his views free from the stereotyped headings. It is not possible to deal with the different types of standard forms in use and the suggestions which are made in this chapter are based on the assumption that the salesman has to compile his report without the help of specific headings.

When considering a general report, as opposed to a report on an individual call, the first and most important matter is the reason for writing the report. The objective should be clear and free from any ambiguities so that the salesman knows what is wanted. Since management require the report it should be the management which defines the objective. Very often management asks for a report on trade and the salesman's activities and the precise objective is left to the salesman. When this happens the salesman, left to his own initiative, should place his objective clearly at the head of the report or, if it deals with several matters, he should put the objective at the head of each section. Only when he has a clear idea of what he is going to write about can the salesman start to prepare his report in a workmanlike way.

A good report is one which gives a clear understanding to the reader and gives an answer to the objective. Reports may contain facts and, as a rule, these will be embodied in the report. If the facts are likely to form a considerable part of the report it may be advisable to place them in a separate appendix but this is unusual in salesmen's reports.

With a clear objective in mind, the salesman should gather all the information that he can and should put it down in note form, preferably on separate sheets of paper or cards. This may seem a tedious process but it will help considerably in constructing the report.

When as much information as possible has been assembled it should be divided carefully and scrupulously into fact and opinion, and the source of each piece of information should be accurately noted. The separation of fact and opinion and the support of each by the source is an invaluable aid to the reader of the report in assessing the importance of the information. For example if the salesman states in his report that one of his leading wholesalers, who is known to be an important and influential man, has advised him that a competitor is about to bring out a new line, the news will probably be accepted as authentic. If, on the other hand, the information comes from a shop assistant in a small, unimportant shop and is not confirmed from any other source, the news will probably be accepted with reservations.

The salesman who quotes opinions without giving sources does himself a disservice and may earn the reputation of being a man who will believe everything he is told without bothering to make reasonable enquiries regarding the accuracy of the information.

When fact and opinion have been separated and sources noted, each item of information should be examined individually within the context of the objective. Any item found to be irrelevant to the objective should be rejected and excluded from the report. This is an important stage in the preparation because few things can make a report so tedious as the inclusion of a lot of irrelevant matter.

A common occurrence in report writing is that salesmen sometimes omit information on the grounds that it is general knowledge and the management are sure to be aware of it. The standard which the salesman can apply is simply, 'Have I included the information in a report before?' If not, it should be put in briefly and clearly.

The stage has now been reached when only relevant information sorted into facts and opinion, with sources, is ready. This should now be arranged in some roughly logical order. The precise order is not of great importance as long as it is reasonably logical and each piece of information follows naturally upon another.

Having progressed so far, the salesman can start to shape or construct his report by setting down the headings and sub-headings which will make up the whole report. There are two simple rules which are worth bearing in mind when writing the report and these are:

1 Always use words that are known and understood. If in doubt consult a dictionary.
2 Use short simple sentences with only one idea in each sentence.

If the procedure outlined above is followed and the two rules applied then writing the report, it will help to make it lucid, logical and understandable. Such reports quickly come to be relied upon by management and the confidence in the salesman who writes them will be increased.

The foregoing remarks apply to general reports which are required by the management but they can also be applied to any special reports which are demanded. General reports often refer to the trade or state of the market and the salesman's activities. This kind of report is dealt with in greater detail below.

Reports on the State of the Market and Salesman's Activities

The method of gathering information is usually the salesman's perception. He should develop a keen observation and take a close interest in the commercial activities on his territory and should always try to check information which is gained secondhand.

The headings and sub-headings which are used in the report will depend upon the objective and the information which has been gathered together. The headings which are set out below are suggested for general reports and can be changed as the occasion warrants.

Market Activities

This heading should cover the general market activities and may include a series of sub-headings which could cover the following subjects.

Mergers

Any mergers or takeover activities which happen on the territory and are of interest to the salesman's trade should be recorded. Mergers and takeovers may be by competitive manufacturers wishing to gain control of wholesale or retail distributive outlets or users to safeguard the sales of their products. They may be the merging of distributors or takeover by wholesalers of retail outlets. Sometimes, although rarely, a large wholesaler may takeover a small manufacturer.

Financial Associations

Occasionally an exchange of financial interest can take place with reciprocal trading benefit between the parties involved. If such an arrangement is made between a competing manufacturer and a distributor, the salesman's company may suffer. In many trades manufacturers have large financial interests in the distributive outlets and the salesman should be alert to discover any extension of these interests.

Associations

Sometimes there are traditional and family associations in the trade and gentlemen's agreements that one company will concentrate on certain kinds of goods and leave other kinds to competitors; sometimes this applies to areas as well.

Promotional Activities of Customers

This kind of activity usually applies in the distributive trades but occasionally a user or manufacturer who buys a salesman's products will want to mention them in his promotions. Sometimes the promotion may be a general one such as for spring cleaning and the manufacturers of detergents, soaps, mops, scrubbing brushes, polishes, paints, etc., will all benefit.

Price cutting

The amount of price cutting which occurs on the territory may be an important piece of information. Details of the outlets which are cutting prices, the products and the actual prices quoted should be included in the report.

Premium offers

Any premium offers which may be either manufacturer or dealer-sponsored should be noted and full details given.

Clearance offers

Some traders seem to hold almost permanent clearance sales and these are often price cutting activities and should be reported. When a limited clearance offer is made the salesman should try to find the reason and the extent of the offers. Some clearances result from an acute shortage of cash and others as a result of overbuying and it is helpful if the salesman can discover the events which led to the decision.

Special needs of customers

These may be unsatisfied needs and too small for a manufacturer to meet profitably. It is worth recording them because if there is a small unsatisfied need on several territories it may, in total, be worth supplying. By noting these needs, and whether they increase or decrease, the salesman may help in the making of management decisions.

General prosperity

This is a difficult matter to gauge. Farmers, for example, are often reputed to be on the brink of bankruptcy. Trade opinions, about prosperity need to be assessed very carefully. Some territories are heavily dependent upon a single industry such as the boot and shoe trade in Leicester, the hotel trades in resort towns, and the pottery trade around Stoke. Fortunately most centres which grew up around a single industry have diversified their commercial interests but a slump in a particular industry can still seriously affect the prosperity on some territories. When this happens, management should be informed.

Dealer or User Reactions

The reactions of customers, whether indirectly from dealers or directly from users, are of considerable importance. By finding out these reactions and reporting them the salesman keeps his management informed of the degree of satisfaction which their products are creating. There are several sub-headings which can be used for recording reactions and these are:

Company policies

It is not suggested that the salesman should canvass opinion by asking bluntly each customer what he thinks of the company policy. If there are any features of company policy which are not popular with some traders the salesman should explain the company point of view and note the customers' reactions. Any changes in policy should be explained fully and carefully and the customer, if he disagrees with them, will almost certainly voice his opinions. The reactions should be included in the salesman's report together with his own views on their strength and possible effect on company trade. If many traders have hostile views the salesman should be careful to watch for any joint approach or joint action by them.

Prices and trade margins

The reaction of dealers and users to prices and margins should be observed, particularly when prices change. Some dealers have campaigned for better margins and have then used them to cut prices. The salesman should be wary of demands in this direction.

The products

The reaction to the product or products is probably the most important point on which to report from customers. Both dealer and user are concerned with product satisfaction and a trouble-free association with or use of it. The reactions should cover saleability in the case of the dealer and, for both dealer and user, should cover performance, design, packaging and any other feature which they wish to comment upon. Sometimes the report should be supported with data and, on occasions, it may be advisable to send in used material to show the effect of wear and tear on performance.

Advertising

The customers' reactions to advertising is of considerable interest to management. When the customer is the user the advertising may be the means which influenced his original purchase. In the case of the dealer, the advertising may have been a major factor in persuading him to become a stockist. Advertising is a subject on which most people have fairly strong views and the salesman should be careful, as in the case of company policy, to explain the company's advertising policy fully and to note reactions. It is possible that during the discussions on advertising a customer may reveal the main reason for purchasing a particular product. If the same reason is given by the majority of customers it may well be that this reason should form the basis of the advertising claims. Occasionally the advertising claims may be ineffective because the claims made, although accurate, do not appear to be presented in a practical and convincing manner and the salesman in reporting his customers' views may help to establish a more satisfactory method.

Sales promotion

The sales promotion activities, like advertising, often give rise to strong views and also to a wide range of suggestions. These should all be recorded and the salesman's comments added so that his opinions of the customers' suggestions become known to his management. If opinions can be supported by facts – for example, that a dealer has increased his sales by twenty per cent as a result of a particular promotion – they should always be included.

One of the difficult tasks of management is to evaluate the benefits of different kinds of promotional activities. The salesman who can provide data to support opinion can render very useful help in this direction.

Credit policy

Dealer and user reactions to credit policy are usually made known to the salesman very quickly if they are hostile. Usually the credit policy in each industry is consistent and is accepted by most dealers.

Delivery arrangements

Management needs to know whether the delivery methods are satisfactory. The goods must not only arrive in a reasonable time but be handled satisfactorily in transit. If it is possible, the salesman should, occasionally, try to be present at the actual delivery of his company's goods. Should delivery problems and queries arise at any time, a salesman with practical knowledge of the method is more likely to be able to deal with them effectively and to report on them accurately.

Service

When there is a service element to the goods which the salesman offers he must, obviously, report on customer reactions. Inefficient service can be a source of extreme irritation to customers and can lose the goodwill which a salesman may have created over a long period of time. Reports on service should, whenever possible, quote full details of any shortcomings and give the names of customers so that appropriate action can be taken.

Distribution of Goods

A particularly important piece of information for management is the number of users or dealers who buy their products. In some industries this information may be easy to acquire. For example, the Census of Distribution report contains details of the number of shops, analysed by certain kinds of trade such as Chemists, Grocers, etc. If the company only supply their goods direct to retail shops, then the number of active accounts can be related to the total number of the same kind.in the country and the percentage stocking the product calculated quite easily.

Consumer products are often supplied both direct to retailers and through wholesalers and there are not always accurate records of the number of users in the country. The investigations necessary for an estimate of the distribution of goods to be made can be complicated.

The salesman will, of course, know accurately how many users and dealers he calls upon and will know which products he sells to each. By consulting his records he can probably quote the kind of information shown in Table 7.1 easily.

Table 7.1

	No. of Direct Accounts	Stockists of Brand A	Percentage Distribution
Chemists			
Wholesalers	2	1	50%
Multiples	4	3	75%
Retailers	150	100	66·6%

This can be done for whatever category of buyer is called upon. It is more difficult when the salesman has to try to relate the number of stockists or users of his products on his territory to the total number of potential stockists or users.

To estimate the number stocking his products may involve his calling upon a sample of dealers who are supplied through a wholesaler or on users who buy from a distributor. Obviously the salesman cannot spend a lot of time checking on stockists but it is helpful if he can discover the total number of potential outlets on his territory by consulting directories or knowledgeable people in the trade. Having ascertained the total potential, the salesman should then make an estimate from his own records, his calls on stockists or users who may buy from middlemen, and from his general enquiries among wholesalers, of the number who stock or use. This figure, as in the table above, can be related to the potential and the percentage distribution for each brand worked out.

The salesman should, preferably, show a percentage figure for distribution in his report or, if not, should show both the potential number of stockists or users and the estimated number of actual stockists or users.

Salesman's Activities

A report which covers the salesman's own activities should always be as factual as possible. Vagueness can very easily be misinterpreted as concealment. The kind of headings which may be helpful to use can best be shown in simple tabular form, as in Table 7.2.

Table 7.2

Grocers	No. of Calls	No. of Orders	% Orders to Calls	Value of Orders £
Retail shops	20	12	60%	720
Multiple shops	5	3	60%	300
Wholesalers	2	1	50%	500
Total	27	16	59%	1520

A simple table can give the factual information of a record of performance which covers the kind of customers visited, the number of calls, the number or orders, the percentage of orders to calls (this may be left for Head Office to calculate) and the value of orders.

Other simple factual information which may be included could deal with any special promotional activities which the salesman has undertaken. Perhaps the number of displays arranged and the location of each, in the case of important sites, could be detailed in the report.

Earlier in the chapter there was a brief mention of the possibility of a report for each call and this kind of report is necessary in some industries. The kind of information which should be shown in a call report is listed below:

1   Name of customer.
2   Address of customer.
3   Delivery address for goods or invoices if different.
4   Name and status of buyer.
5   Nature of customer's business.
6   Size and type of customer's business.
    (For example, shop or factory employing twenty people and formed as a partnership or limited company.)
7   Date of call.
8   Products or equipment in use or in stock.
9   Action to be taken such as submission of designs, estimates or information.
10 Details of order obtained if applicable.
11 Any general remarks of interest.

The call report is usually required in those industries where follow-up action is considered necessary from Head Office. The kind of action coming into this category would be where a design, an estimate, a model or a sample has to be submitted. Sometimes call reports are necessary where capital equipment is sold, so that confirmatory quotations or follow-up letters can be sent.

Competition

A report on competitive activities may quite easily and conveniently be included as a main heading in the general report on the state of the market. It is dealt with separately because, so often, salesmen are called upon to send in special reports on competitive situations and it is a very important part of the salesman's work to observe the competitive activity.

Many salesmen are expected to report at regular intervals but if any item of urgent information arises, particularly in regard to competition, it should be reported to management immediately.

When a report on competition is being compiled, the following headings may be helpful.

Products

A description of new or modified products should be given and a sample should be sent if this is practicable. The dealers' or users' reactions to the performance and saleability should be quoted, if known, but often the product may not have been on offer long enough for these to be other than initial reactions.

Packaging

A complete package should be sent to Head Office if possible. If not, packaging details should be given covering the type of container used, any special features such as pilfer proof checks, easy to pour devices or after use value, and the number of items in each container.

Prices

As full details as possible should be given. Many salesmen have sufficiently friendly relations with some of their customers for them to be able to obtain this information quite easily and without any embarrassment. Sometimes competitive price lists are readily available and, if so, one of them should be sent with the report.

Terms and Credit

The terms of trading and conditions should be noted and, if possible, the length of credit granted. It may be difficult to obtain satisfactory information on this point as a company's credit policy is often varied to meet different needs.

Advertising

The simplest way to report press or magazine advertising is to send in the publication containing the advertisement. For other forms of advertising, a brief description of the claims and copy and the times of appearance, if on television, or the location of the hoardings for poster advertising, should suffice. It is not suggested that the precise location of each hoarding site should be detailed but information such as 'seen on a hoarding in Halifax' should suffice.

Sales promotion

Any details, particularly if they can be supported by leaflets or display cards, should be sent in. If it is possible to obtain trade or user reactions to the schemes this should also be passed on as well.

Turnover

With competitive activity it is difficult to obtain meaningful information on sales when the product is a new one. Often a friendly dealer or user may volunteer his own figures and as time passes they will become more valuable. In the case of an established competitive product the details of turnover can be a very important piece of information. Extreme tact and discretion is necessary and a salesman who is too persistent in trying to obtain details may meet a very serious rebuff.

Sales methods

The methods used by competitors' sales forces are worth reporting upon. The points to cover are whether sales are made direct to the user, to retail and or multiple and wholesale distributors or any combination of these. If the sales arguments used and the methods of presenting the product can be discovered, this can also be very helpful.

Delivery arrangements

The method of making deliveries may be a factor in determining the success of competitive marketing and the salesman may find interesting information in this category. Are the goods delivered by the competitors' own transport, by a haulier, or are they collected? The degree of satisfaction of the buyer should be noted and recorded in the report.

Service

If there is a service element to competitive goods this should be reported upon and the buyer's reactions recorded, with particular attention to any shortcomings or advantages which may exist. Many buyers pay considerable attention to the standard of the service facilities.

Distribution of goods

When it is possible for the salesman to make a similar estimate of the percentage distribution of a competitor's goods as suggested in the section on general reports, he should include it. With a new product this may change rapidly and the salesman will probably want to bring his estimates up to date occasionally.

Reports on Specific Market Enquiries

When a special report is required the Sales Manager usually specifies the subjects which are to be covered. Sometimes a salesman may be asked merely for a report on a product or a market not currently associated with his own company's activities.

A salesman faced with such a demand must be resourceful and try to place himself in the position of the Sales Manager and think of the kind of information he would want to have.

The general background of a market would probably include:

1 Samples of the product if practicable.
2 A list of the kind of outlets or firms using or stocking the products.

3 The sales methods used.

4 The advertising claims.

5 Sales promotional activities.

6 Dealers' and or users' opinions of products in regard to performance and saleability.

7 The prices and trade margins.

8 The progress of the market (whether sales are increasing or decreasing).

9 An estimate of the total sales of the brand and type of product on the salesman's territory.

10 Any information on delivery arrangements, service and percentage distribution of goods.

Some of this information may be difficult to obtain but, if most of the salesmen employed by a company were successful in their investigations, a thorough and useful market report could be built up by the management.

The composition of reports has been dealt with in considerable detail and, to some salesmen, it may seem to have been overstressed. The methods and suggestions outlined above can be implemented easily, provided the original preparation stages are carefully followed. The most important factors in report-writing are to have a clear objective and to make a thorough preparation. If these principles are used, the actual writing of the report follows as a natural, logical action which can be carried through simply.

Records

Record keeping by the salesman is an essential part of his work. Well-kept records provide an excellent memory and a salesman who consults his record cards before each call can face his buyer with the confidence that he has up-to-date knowledge of the business transacted.

Some of the information which a salesman should record has been mentioned in the section dealing with call reports on individual calls. The salesman's records should provide a more comprehensive background than the individual call report. Most companies have standard record cards and, since they vary considerably, some of the information given below may not necessarily apply to every industry.

The record card should preferably be pre-printed with lines and columns to suit the individual requirements of the company concerned. The kind of information which should be recorded is set out below:

1 Name and address of customer.

2 Addresses for the delivery of goods and invoices if different from above.

3 Name and status of buyer.

4 Early closing day or special buying times.

5 Trade classification (Toy Manufacturer, Retail or Wholesale Confectioner, etc.).

6 Terms classification (Wholesale, Retail or the rate of discount). N.B. This information will probably be in code.

7 Credit rating (probably in code).

8 Ruled columns for the date of call, order number, details of the goods sold and their values.

9 Space for general remarks, which would include size and type of business and buying habits.

It is a common practice to use simple codes for such information as the terms classification and credit rating. This precaution is taken because salesmen often carry their record cards with them and in case of accidental loss the information will not be disclosed to the finder of the card.

The kind of codes which can be used are easy to remember and typical examples could be:

Wholesale terms	A	Credit	limit	of	£1,000	O
Multiple terms	B	"	"	"	£750	P
Retail terms	C	"	"	"	£500	Q
5% off list price	D	"	"	"	£400	R
10% " " "	E	"	"	"	£300	S
15% " " "	F	"	"	"	£200	T
20% " " "	G	"	"	"	£100	U
		"	"	"	£50	V

[Record card]

Name	E.C. Day ....
Address	Trade Classification ....
Address for goods/invoices	Terms ....
Name of buyer	C.R. ....

Remarks:–

Date	O/No.	Goods Sold	£	p.	Remarks

C.R. is an abbreviation for Credit Rating. Any special notes about the account would be entered above the ruled columns. The remarks column could be used for any information relating to the individual orders booked or as a reminder for matters to be discussed at a subsequent call.

The reverse side of the card would be printed with ruled columns only, so that one card would last for a reasonable time for each customer.

Record cards should be kept in journey order so that during the working day the salesman is able to find his cards easily. Methodical filing, in journey order, simplifies journey planning and the salesman can make amendments to his journeys easily by transferring cards and inserting new ones as necessary.

The Essentials of Reporting and Records

Salesmen should remember the purpose of reports and records. Reports are required by management so that it will have an accurate knowledge of the subject reported upon. Facts and opinions should be separated whenever possible and sources of information quoted so that management can assess its value. The salesman should try to view his reports through management's eyes and bear in mind that good management decisions can only be made when they are based on accurate information.

Similarly, accurate, well kept, up-to-date records can make a valuable contribution to the salesman's operating efficiency.

8 Variations in Selling Situations

A salesman has to adapt himself to the moods of customers and present his sales arguments accordingly; he must also be very much aware of the different kinds of techniques to use with different types of buyers.

When analysing the main buying interests or motives of buyers the salesman will quickly see that not only will main buying interests vary between individuals, there will also be fundamental differences of interest between different types of buyers. These fundamental differences should be analysed by the salesman and he should work out the techniques which he needs to deal with the various situations which he encounters.

Customers can be divided into several broad categories each of which has a common interest, such as manufacturers, wholesalers, retailers and users. There is an additional kind of selling which can cut across these broad categories and which is best described as technical selling.

The differences between the main buying interests of these broad categories will be analysed and the salesman should carry out a similar analysis when dealing with his own customers.

Manufacturers

Manufacturers who use the salesman's product may be described as users but in the context of these remarks this category of manufacturers is intended to apply only to manufacturers who buy the products for use in their manufacturing process. The kind of example which illustrates this point is the confectioner who buys flour and other products to make cakes which he then sells. Other kinds of user are dealt with in a later section as a separate category.

Most of the products which are bought for use in manufacturing processes are raw materials from which the end product is made, packing materials, machinery to carry out the manufacturing processes and the tools and equipment necessary for servicing and handling machinery and goods. These types of products make up the main buying demands during the manufacturing stage.

The main buying interests in relation to these products will probably be expressed by executives from specialized departments such as production, maintenance, research or the laboratory for quality control and transport for handling.

When the main buying interests become specialized, as they often do when selling these kinds of products, the salesman should try to see the departmental executive whose advice will be sought by the buyer. This may be difficult and the buyer may feel that the salesman is trying to go behind his back. Extreme tact is necessary in such cases and the salesman should be very careful to make the buyer aware that his sole purpose is to learn of the needs and operating conditions first hand and that any negotiations will be conducted through the buyer.

Once the salesman has gained access to the responsible executive he should conduct himself with the utmost circumspection and do nothing which can upset the relationship between himself and the buyer or the buyer and the executive. His enquiries and interest should be confined to studying the process through which his product will pass or the jobs it will have to do and to finding the standards of performance which are required.

The needs of the specialist departments are likely to be simple ones to establish but may be difficult to achieve. The production department will probably be satisfied if the product meets the specifications which have been agreed and is consistent. Products or raw materials which are consistent in their standards usually give trouble-free performance and enable the production line to flow smoothly without irritating stoppages. Meeting a buyer's specification is satisfactory but sometimes products which are far superior may be troublesome because the machinery which handles them may have to be adjusted to deal with varying standards and this can cause serious production delays.

The production department will also require delivery of the goods on time. In a large and complicated production unit the production schedule may demand regular weekly deliveries of certain raw materials or component parts. Lack of storage space and the desire to reduce the investment in stocks to the lowest possible level are powerful reasons for some buyers insisting upon a regular delivery programme designed to meet the production schedule.

Machinery which is sold to the production department will not only have to meet the performance standards which have been demanded but will be expected to have a high efficiency rating. On a production line the overall efficiency is that of the least efficient machine and any one machine which slows up production may have to be replaced. Often a machine with a high performance that is capable of working at a faster rate than the maximum required becomes a nuisance because it develops technical faults and has to be adjusted, say, once every hour. This drop in efficiency may mean an operational time of 55 minutes in every 60 minutes. Five minutes in each hour would be lost and the efficiency rating of ninety-two per cent might be too low.

The versatility of the machinery might be a factor which could appeal to a production executive. A machine which is capable of doing different jobs can be of immense benefit when the production is intermittent and also for emergency use during breakdowns.

The availability of spare parts and the service facilities will be important requirements for the production executive. The salesman should assess the importance of all the needs of the production department and he can then try to establish the suitability of his product to meet the needs.

The maintenance department may have different needs and their requirements may be limited to the servicing and repair of machinery. Their anxieties may be about the accessibility of the working parts of machinery, the extent to which material used during manufacture affects the parts of the machinery and the frequency at which maintenance has to be carried out. The speed at which repairs can be done and the degree of technical knowledge required are other factors. If the salesman's company provides an after sales service of a technical nature it is a good technique to introduce the buyer's maintenance executive to the salesman's technician. They will be able to talk over common problems and understand each other's needs.

The needs of the research department or laboratory will probably be expressed in a written specification and the customer's quality control will be based on this. A salesman's contact with a research department or laboratory may not be an essential part of the sales presentation in many industries. Very often the contacts made in this direction are best limited to the establishment of confidence. The salesman should take pains to get a precise specification from the buyer, should try to establish the nature of the tests which are made to check that the specification has been met and should provide as much evidence as possible of his company's capabilities to produce a satisfactory product.

The transport department may have only one requirement and that is that the goods should be packed in a sufficiently strong container to ensure safe delivery. In such instances an assurance that a 'rail certified carton' is used will probably be enough. This standard, which means that the board used in the manufacture of the container is of a certain strength, is accepted by the railway authorities and is in general use. The transport department may become deeply involved when the goods are unusual in size, shape or weight and have special storage requirements. Some goods have to be stored at certain temperatures and others may carry a high insurance or explosive risk and have to be stored away from other goods. Scented goods should be kept well away from some food products such as cheese, bacon and flour because the latter group can pick up strong odours as well as impart them.

Where possible the salesman should try to satisfy the individual specialist needs and he should be able to increase his goodwill with the buyer in doing so. If his attitude throughout these enquiries is one of seeking information for the sole purpose of satisfying the various requirements he will be reassuring the buyer and establishing confidence. The salesman is helping to protect the buyer by ascertaining the needs and then formally making claims to meet them. Only a salesman without any integrity would ever dare to go to such trouble and then make false claims.

The more pains which are taken by the salesman, the more he will establish himself as a man of integrity.

When the various specialists' needs have been met there are still the buyer's needs to be considered. The buyer will, obviously, be interested in satisfying the specialist's needs because his own reputation is concerned. In addition, he may have other needs such as costs. The cost of the product may be part of the prime cost of the goods which the buyer's company is making and the profitability of the company may depend to an important extent on the shrewdness of the buyer.

The salesman should meet the specialists' needs through the buyer because in satisfying the specialists he, at the same time, satisfies the buyer. Finally, the salesman should relate the advantages and benefits of his product to the price which he quotes.

This section should be read in conjunction with Chapter 9, Selling to Industry.

Wholesalers

Wholesalers have quite different buying interests from manufacturers in the products which they buy. By definition wholesalers buy large quantities and sell smaller quantities. They also provide services which go with 'breaking bulk'.

The main interests are concerned with the profit on the goods which they handle and the rate of stock turn. Profit, for the wholesaler, is the margin of profit on one article multiplied by the number of articles which he sells.

A high profit per article with a low rate of stock turn is usually much less interesting, as a business proposition, to a wholesaler than a low profit per article with a high rate of stock turn. In the latter case he can use his capital more frequently and, therefore, has more opportunities of making a profit in each trading year.

A wholesaler's main buying interest is to use his capital as frequently as possible to buy goods, sell them and buy again. If he can perform this cycle frequently he will both provide his retail customers with a quick service of fresh goods and increase his profitability.

The wholesaler has other buying interests and these include his concern for speedy deliveries, the amount of storage space required, the amount and duration of the credit allowed, the storage conditions which goods may require and the extent of the service which he must supply to his customers.

The salesman needs to investigate each of these interests carefully and consider how he can meet them. Another matter which may be of joint concern for both the wholesaler and the salesman is that of packaging. In some trades an increasing number of wholesalers are refusing to break bulk and will only despatch complete packages to retailers. Many manufacturers have revised their packages to contain only one dozen units so that all distributors can handle their products as expeditiously as possible.

Apart from the main interests mentioned above, which apply to most wholesalers, there are individual requirements which the salesman should examine carefully. He should try to discover as much information as possible about each individual wholesale customer. In most trades there are variations in the stock lists of different wholesalers; most will stock the popular lines but individual wholesalers may often specialize in some part of the trade. The salesman should try to discover the kind of retailer served and the type of trade which he conducts. By discovering the frequency of call made by the wholesaler's salesman, the manufacturer's salesman will learn the kind of service the retailer is getting.

Through continual contact the manufacturer's salesman will learn the rate of stock turn of the wholesaler and will be able to regulate his sales to him so that the wholesaler has regular deliveries of fresh stock.

A service which most wholesalers find acceptable is the booking of transfer orders. These are orders which the manufacturer's salesman books for goods which will be delivered by a wholesaler nominated by the retailer who has given the order. If the booking of transfer orders is part of his company's policy the salesman can demonstrate practically the value of the service which his company offers to wholesalers.

Another service which the salesman can offer is that of sales aids and display material. These may be given to the wholesaler for distribution to his customers but this is not always the best method. If the salesman can deliver the material and arrange the displays himself the results will usually be better because he will be more conscious of the display requirements of his company.

Retailers

The interests of the retailer are very similar to those of the wholesaler. The retailer is concerned with buying large quantities (small by wholesale standards) and retailing them to the public in smaller quantities, probably in single units.

The retailer's profit is calculated in the same way as that for the wholesaler; it is the margin of profit on one article multiplied by the number of articles sold. Like the wholesaler, the retailer tries to turn his stock over as frequently as possible. The retailer has other interests and these include, as for the wholesaler, speedy and regular deliveries, limitations of storage space, the credit which he is allowed and the service which he has to give to his customers.

The special interests of the retailer to which the salesman should pay attention are the presentation of the product to the public, the package and impulse appeal of the product.

The presentation and impulse appeal will include the design, colour and general appearance of the product and these are of particular importance where the product is mostly bought by housewives. The influence on product and package design by supermarkets and self-service stores has been significant and any salesman who calls upon them regularly will know the importance to the retailers of package design and product presentation.

Retailers are also interested in knowing the extent and nature of the advertising support which the product receives. With new products retailers often want to know when the advertising will commence and ask to see advance 'pulls' (actual copies of the advertisement prepared in advance from the printer's blocks).

One manufacturer, knowing the retailers' interest in the advertising support, supplied each of his representatives with a cassette player and cassettes. At each call the salesman played the tape which reproduced the sound track, complete with music, of a television commercial which was to appear later in the year.

The display material which can be supplied is another retail interest and the ingenuity and skill which has been utilized in devising attractive and practical displays again testifies to the importance of presenting goods in an appealing manner. Many display pieces incorporate storage units and sometimes act as dispensers from which the customer can help himself.

The salesman should study the needs of the retailer and, as for the wholesaler, should try to estimate the rate of stock turn and then sell a quantity which will meet the requirements of a reasonably quick turnover of goods. A wholesaler's salesman who calls on retailers can probably promise regular and frequent deliveries and, in this respect, offer a better service than the manufacturer's salesman.

Users

Users have been placed in a separate category and are defined for the purpose of this section as customers who use goods or services but not as part of their manufacturing processes. Practically every company uses typewriters, stationery, motor-cars, office furniture and many other goods which may be bought direct from manufacturers, from wholesalers or from retailers.

If it is possible the salesman should make direct contact with the users and should try to obtain their comments first hand. Sometimes it may not be possible to get first hand information but the salesman should make the attempt and, if he cannot get it, he should try to obtain opinions from the closest source to the user as possible. The salesman may need to exercise considerable tact to avoid any appearance of trying to undermine the buyer's authority. This may be done by stressing the importance which the salesman's company attaches to first hand information as a means of safeguarding the buyer by ensuring that the user's needs are met more accurately.

When the user's needs have been established, the salesman can relate his sales presentation to them and whether they refer to performance, economy or any of the other main buying interests he can do so with some practical experience of them.

Most users will be concerned with performance and economy but whatever the main interests the salesman should be fully conversant with the data and able to make any calculations to support his claims. It is more effective if any claims can be applied to the user's business and the figures used in savings calculations taken from the user's own experience.

When the user and the buyer are the same person, the presentation of the salesman's case will be easier because of the buyer's practical understanding of the situation. If the user and buyer are separate individuals the salesman will find it advantageous to satisfy the user through the buyer because, as in the case of selling to manufacturers, the buyer will take part in the process of satisfaction.

Technical Selling

This is a specialized kind of selling and usually the salesman is technically qualified or has received some technical training. There are no limitations on the categories of buyers and they may be manufacturers, wholesalers, retailers or users. The kinds of products which are classed as 'speciality' or 'industrial' are industrial paints and finishes, fertilizers, insecticides and herbicides, when sold to agriculturists (as opposed to consumer packs sold through retail outlets), hand tools for tool merchants and similar products which require technical knowledge in their application.

In some cases the salesman may be engaged and then expected to train himself, though this is not a very satisfactory situation. If he becomes faced with this problem the salesman must, of course, try to equip himself, as quickly as possible, with all the technical knowledge that he is likely to need. He may be able to do this by questioning technicians in the employ of his company, by study, and by contact with his customers. Although all salesmen will probably learn something from their customers, the acquisition of the rudiments of technical knowledge from customers by a salesman who is supposed to know something about his product is not recommended.

On occasions the salesman is virtually a technical adviser to his customers, and at other times, he may be the link between the customers and the trained technician who is available to give advice to them. He must, therefore, take a deep interest in his customers' problems and be prepared to study them in detail. Visits to the customers' workshops may be necessary and many technical salesmen carry overalls and tool kits in case they are faced with a practical problem.

The technical salesman should be very careful to keep within the limits of his authority to speak on technical matters. He should also realise the limitations which are imposed by the amount of knowledge which he possesses. A technical salesman will create far more confidence if he frankly admits that a problem is beyond his authority or his knowledge and calls in an expert. The dangers of a salesman trying to handle a problem which is beyond his resources and failing are too obvious to need more than a passing mention.

The good technical salesman who goes to the trouble to learn his customers' problems and treats them as his own usually becomes closely allied to his customers and almost takes on the role of a consultant. As confidence is built up he forges a link between himself and his customer which has the strength of reliability, trust, technical ability and integrity.

Flexibility in Selling

The sales approach needs to be modified according to the kind of buyers encountered. Most salesmen meet a variety of buyers from different trade categories and they will improve their sales performances if they recognize the disparate interests of the categories and adapt the sales approach and presentation accordingly. Such action by the salesman is an extension of the requirement to ascertain the buyer's needs.

Forethought and preparation based on a knowledge of trade interests are sure to develop a greater flexibility and a more resourceful and competent salesman.

9 Selling to Industry

Most of the previous chapters have been devoted to the qualifications of salesmen, the principles and techniques of professional salesmanship and the self-organization by salesmen to manage their territories. However, salesmanship is practised in a wide variety of situations. The news-vendor selling newspapers on a street corner practises salesmanship, so does the team of highly qualified technicians selling an industrial turnkey project to a foreign government. As can be expected, the skills and techniques employed by a team of technicians are complex and must be well organized.

In this chapter, some of the special problems which are encountered in the specialized field of selling to industry are discussed and analysed. Suggestions are made of the kind of sales approach which can be used successfully.

First of all, the industrial field is a vast one. It embraces heavy engineering where often each order is subject to competitive tender and includes a design element; by contrast, it also includes the mass production of simple components which may be manufactured on a sub-contracting basis for supply to, say, a motor vehicle manufacturer (who in reality is an assembler).

The kind of products bought by industrial enterprises will include raw materials, packaging materials, machines, spare parts, a wide range of consumable items and a variety of services. Each of these has several sub-categories which require careful study.

Raw Materials

Almost all manufacturing industries use raw materials of one kind or another. At one time, many industries bought in crude raw materials which they processed to produce the semi-refined or refined material to use in their manufacturing processes. Many crude raw materials came and still come from what are often referred to as 'developing countries'. Africa, for example, exports mineral oil, timber, cocoa, coffee, vegetable oil, essences, gold, diamonds, chrome, copper, spices, fruits and vegetables plus hundreds of other products. These are often imported by 'developed' countries where they are refined or processed to become finished articles. Perhaps the best known crude raw material is mineral oil – the crude oil was originally exported and refined in developed countries and the refined produce was sold back to the original country of source for use as petrol.

It can readily be understood that the developing countries wish to enjoy the 'added value' themselves. Almost every oil-producing country now has its own oil refineries alongside the sources of crude oil but the refining capacity is insufficient to handle all the 'crude' which is produced. The same procedure of refining or partially processing at source is continuing in many industries and countries throughout the world.

Crude raw materials

Raw materials bought by industrial enterprises may still be in the crude state and they are usually sold by sample or by specification. If the crude raw material is bulky, it can readily be appreciated that the transport in bulk over long distances to a refinery is a costly operation. Crude raw materials are used less and less frequently in modern industry. The technological advances in industrial processing demand consistent material at the input stage.

The buyer of crude raw material demands, as a rule, either a sample for control purposes or a written statement specifying the percentage content of the key elements in the bulk material. The specification may also limit the amount of 'contaminating' material which is acceptable. Distillers of scotch whisky and brewers buy high quality barley to make malt and the moisture content of the barley is critical. Consignments of barley are usually controlled at point of despatch and again at delivery, to check on the moisture content, and the contract will usually include penalty clauses. The importance of specifying the limits of 'contaminating' ingredients can be appreciated when one finds that high grade barley can be sold at more than twice the price of moisture-contaminated barley which may be disposed of for animal feeding. There are parallel situations in most industries.

In addition to the specification, the buyer will also be concerned with delivery times. The purchase order often includes a delivery schedule which specifies the quantities and dates by which delivery is required. As before, there may be penalty clauses for non-compliance. Price is obviously a factor but may be secondary to specification and delivery times. There is usually a long lead time in the delivery and processing of crude raw materials and it is customary for long-term contracts to be agreed between buyers and sellers. The contracts are likely to cover at least a season in the case of seasonal raw materials and usually twelve months for non-seasonal raw materials.

The salesman must take care to ascertain the buyer's main buying interests and, particularly, be aware of seasonal fluctuations in supply, demand, prices and quality.

Semi-refined and semi-processed raw materials

The raw material has already been partially processed. The slag heaps which surround coal mines are visual evidence of a simple 'refining' process. With semi-refined or processed raw materials, the specifications are likely to be more precise than those used for crude raw materials. The standards and methods of testing and controlling are likely to be universally accepted within the industry. Similarly, the penalty clauses are likely to be standard. The buyers of semi-refined material will want delivery according to a prepared time-table.

In the case of semi-refined products, the lead time for supply will usually be less than in the case of crude raw materials and contracts tend to be of shorter duration. The salesman, therefore, must be well grounded on the subjects of specifications and delivery schedules but he must also be ready and able to sell 'spot' to buyers who require quick delivery.

Refined, processed raw materials

Industrial processors who manufacture in quantity or 'mass' are usually buyers of refined raw materials. Mass production necessitates consistency of material. For example, bulk consignments of timber which have not been adequately 'seasoned' will create problems in the furniture industry. Similarly, in the food industry, bulk consignments of tomato puree, fruit juice or any other concentrate which falls below standard will, unless controlled at point of intake to the factory, cause problems later on.

The specifications for refined raw materials will be precise and the tolerances will be minimal. Delivery schedules are likely to be strict and the lead time will be shorter than for crude or semi-refined raw materials.

The industrial buyers will want to keep their investment in stocks of raw materials as low as possible and it may be part of the buying/ selling negotiations for the supplier to keep a guaranteed quantity as a reserve stock of raw material on behalf of the buyer.

The salesman will need to know and understand the specifications of his buyers, their delivery schedules and also the conditions which may lead to demands on the guaranteed reserve stock. One of his important duties may be to give 'early warning' to his Head Office of a possible demand on the reserve stocks.

Auxiliary raw materials, catalysts

Many raw materials are subjected to complex processes. Some of them were mentioned in Chapter 2. But it is in the 'process' industries, where manufacturing is a continuous, non-stop process which is only stopped to carry out 'down-time' maintenance, that one finds numerous examples of complexity. Examples of process industries are petro-chemicals, some plastics and some chemical re-generation plants. Some of the process industries and also some non-process industries use raw materials (usually chemicals) which act as catalysts or which produce re-actions and changes in form and substance of the basic raw material.

The chemicals which are used may, for example, be acids or alkalis and during the process they suffer dilution and lose strength. However, the diluted solutions are rarely thrown away but are 'recovered' and brought up to the required strength by the addition of concentrates. With some chemicals, recovery, fortification and re-use can continue almost indefinitely.

The salesman needs to know and understand the processes of his customers and be able to relate the 'qualities' of his product to them. He needs also to know and understand the recommended 'recovery' techniques.

Effluents

The current pre-occupation with pollution has drawn the attention of the general public to one of the problems of industry. The disposal of effluent has been a problem for generations and most manufacturers who dispose of toxic effluents have had long-established treatment procedures. During the last few decades, industrial chemistry has been 'revolutionized'. Many industries which were based on natural raw materials are now based on chemicals and synthetics. Two examples come to mind. Cotton has been largely replaced by synthetic fibres and paints are now largely made from chemicals.

The chemical 'revolution' has brought new effluent problems and the salesman of products which may have undesirable effluent characteristics should be able to discuss the problem and make recommendations which will provide a satisfactory solution to his customers.

Packaging Material

Articles produced in a factory may be packaged immediately in the package which will carry them to the ultimate consumer. But many products are stored in 'temporary' packages and may be repacked later. The latter procedure applies particularly to components and small items such as nuts, bolts, screws, and washers.

The types of packaging material may vary and sometimes special packaging for cold climates or tropical climates is necessary. The term packaging is often limited to the container but labelling is also part of the packaging function. The label is sometimes the package – a skein of wool carries a label which holds the skein together. Some of the types of packaging material and the situations in which they are used are described below.

Bulk packaging

Packaging in bulk is common to most industries. Nails are sold 'in bulk' to consumers, by weight from retail hardware shops and ironmongers. Flour is sold in sacks or in special bulk vehicles to bakers and confectioners. Cement is delivered ready-mixed, in specially constructed vehicles, to construction sites. Malt whisky is shipped in bulk containers to many parts of the world where it is 'blended' to produce blended whisky. Engineering components are, similarly, shipped all over the world.

Bulk containers have been rationalized and the impetus towards rationalization has been helped by the development of container handling. Standard sizes of containers are being used increasingly and this trend has been accelerated by the growth of mechanical handling and palletization.

Bulk packaging is linked to handling methods and bulk packages are designed to protect and sometimes to publicize. They should always be designed for easy, safe, economical handling of the product.

The salesman of bulk packaging material must often commence his contact with a prospective customer by a research into his packaging needs. His role has become almost that of a consultant and the information he should try to obtain about his customer's bulk packaging will include:

1 the product's normal keeping qualities or its shelf life;
2 in the case of metal products or machines, the risk of rust or seizure of parts through non-use;
3 the environment in which the product is used;
4 whether or not the container can be re-sealed without adversely affecting the product;
5 whether or not the container will need to be moved frequently and the personnel and lifting facilities available;
6 the pros and cons of incorporating special devices for:

(a) ease of pouring
(b) ease of re-sealing
(c) attaching to a magazine to 'feed' a machine
(d) measuring and counting usage or residue
(e) ease of handling.

7 any special circumstances concerning:
(a) storage
(b) humidity
(c) toxicity
(d) odours – gives off or absorbs.

An example of the close affinity between bulk packaging and handling (mechanical or manual) is the roll pallet. This piece of equipment is a pallet with wheels which can be handled either with a fork-lift truck or manually. It is a 'bulk packaging container with wheels'. It has substantial wire cage sides and can be fitted with a top. Sides and top are easily removable but can also be padlocked for security. The goods may be loaded, in bulk or in cartons, on to the roll pallet which can be pushed by hand or carried by a fork-lift truck and loaded into a vehicle. A vehicle with a tail lift unit can load the roll pallet without difficulty. The vehicles may be equipped with tracks to take the roll pallet wheels and with locking devices to secure the pallets during transit. The system is widely used by supermarket chains to service their branches. When the roll pallets are unloaded at the branch they are almost always handled manually.

Consumer packaging

Consumer packaging has also undergone revolutionary changes. The introduction of packaging films and 'heat-shrink' techniques whereby the film provides a sealed coating, which approximately follows the contours of the product, is a typical example of protection plus promotion. The product is protected within its transparent wrapper and is fully visible. A similar technique is used in the bottling industry. Wet 'shrink-on' cellulose seals are used as a secondary closure on some bottled products. The seal can be printed by a brenthate process and the seal takes on the contours of the bottle top and neck. Expensive recording equipment and cameras are packed in moulded polystyrene which protects the goods and can be used as a display tray. These are all typical examples of the developments which have lifted consumer packaging from its primary role of protection to that of promotion.

It is in the field of consumer packaging that labelling plays an important part. The salesman of consumer packaging material must obviously look well beyond the functional role of his product. He must also be aware of the use to which his product will be put. The can salesman, for example, sold cans to food and other manufacturers. The labels to 'dress' the cans were sold by designers and printers. However, the development of lithoprinted plate has changed the can salesman into one who also sells designs and the printing services of his company. A dramatically-designed can label may make a significant impact for a newly launched product.

Apart from the design aspect of packages, the salesman may also need production know-how. One of the reasons for using 'one-trip' bottles in some sectors of the beverage industry is that returned bottles will not all belong to the same manufacturer's batch, and the intricate precision machines which cap and label the bottles are adjusted to deal with bottles which all have identical measurements, which in practice means from the same batch. Some bottles even have a 'lug' at the base which is used to self-position the bottle precisely on the bottling line so that 'neck', 'shoulder' and 'body' labels can be placed on the bottles symmetrically.

A salesman in the consumer packaging field needs to be a 'jack of all trades'. It is perhaps a slight exaggeration to give such a description because it is rare to find salesmen who sell all kinds of packages such as glass bottles, metal cans, cardboard cartons, paper bags, tubes of various materials plus the great variety of plastic packages. Salesmen usually, are confined to one kind of material and there are few organizations which manufacture packages in a variety of materials. Nevertheless, even when limited to one kind of material the salesman needs to be knowledgeable about a wide range of production practices and fully aware of how the packages he sells can be used to promote the products which they contain. That alone is sufficient to develop his versatility.

Machinery

The variety of machines used in industry is such that machinery exhibitions are generally limited to specific types of machines or for the machines of a particular industrial sector. Examples are, Materials Handling, Ceramic Plant and Machinery, Pneumatics and Hydraulics, Leather and Leather Machinery etc. etc. It would be impossible to group together, in any one exhibition centre, a sample of the machines used in every industry. Some idea of the variety of machines in common, everyday use can be gleaned from the short list below.

Metal-working industry

Drills
Lathes
Milling machines
Grinders
Cutting machines
Broaching machines
Bending machines
Wire and tube drawing machines
Tube manipulating machines
Buffing machines
Numerically controlled machine tools

Wood-working industry

Drills
Saws
Combination machines
Sanding machines
Grinders
Polishers
Trimming machines
Bevelling machines
Joint cutting machines

Bottling industry

Filling machines
Sterilization units
Bottle washing machines
Capping machines
Labelling machines
Packing machines

The above, very short, list gives a limited range of the types of machines and there are numerous models of each type.

The machinery salesman has to know his 'machine' in detail. He should know its performance under different working conditions, its limitations and, of course, its shortcomings. He also needs to know the problems of the users of his machine and how he can help overcome them. He must be able to demonstrate or arrange for an 'on site' visit to see the machine in operation and he must be conversant with preventive maintenance, down-time maintenance, and spare part requirements.

While many machines are sold as individual units, there are others which may be sold in groups. Numerically controlled machine tools are generally installed to equip a whole workshop. Similarly, machines may have to be linked on a production line where the 'speed' of the slowest machine governs the speed of the line. It is sometimes necessary to break a production line to accommodate a 'slow' machine. Two or more 'slow' machines will be installed in 'parallel' and the line divided so that each machine deals with the items which it can handle. The 'broken line' is then reformed to take up the desired speed.

When machines are installed, either in parallel or as part of a production line, the salesman needs to be familiar with the production methods so that he can explain how his machine will fit into the line.

Change parts

Many machines are versatile and perform several different operations. Wood working combination machines are made in various models and some models can perform up to seven different machine functions. The change of function is normally achieved by using 'change parts'. A simple example is the hand tool which can accommodate different size screwdriver blades, a gimlet or a pricker.

Part of the salesman's product knowledge will include knowing the range of change parts, their functions and the time necessary to make the change. Some machines may need to be cleaned out before change parts are replaced and the down time may be a crucial factor which could affect the outcome of sales negotiations.

Purchase arrangements

The purchase of industrial machinery, in the case of small inexpensive machines such as a mechanical saw, can be financed out of working capital. But often, the purchase of machinery is a major capital investment requiring loan capital. The suppliers of the machinery may arrange long-term credit, suitably secured, and payment will be made over the credit period.

Some suppliers of machinery, particularly when the machine has special or unique characteristics which are patented, do not sell their machines outright. They are supplied on a 'royalty' basis which is calculated on the output. A sealed measuring device is attached to the machine and the royalty is payable at so much per unit produced. The royalty method reinforces the patent protection and often the patent holder will not allow the machine to be made under licence.

Leasing has become increasingly popular and applies to all kinds of machinery. With leasing it is usual for a fixed sum to be paid on a monthly basis whether or not the machine is used.

A machinery salesman must be familiar with the credit and payment policies of his company and be able and empowered to tailor them to the needs of his customers.

Plant hire

Plant hire may be considered as an alternative purchase arrangement, akin to leasing, but it merits special treatment because it has developed and become a permanent part of some industrial sectors. In the construction and civil engineering industries, plant hire probably accounts for the major part of machine utilization. It differs from royalty and leasing arrangements in that it is usually limited to short-term operations. The kind of machinery which makes up the major part of the plant hire business is that used in construction, such as earth moving equipment – dump trucks, dumpers (motorized wheelbarrows) graders, bull-dozers, tractors, concrete mixers, stone crushers, hoists, mobile generators, compressors, pneumatic drills and many other similar machines.

The projects in which plant hire machinery is used are generally of comparatively short duration, can vary (exceptionally) from one day to several months, and are usually localized. On completion of the contract the machinery will be taken back by the plant hire company, re-conditioned and serviced and hired out to another contractor.

The salesman of plant hire is selling a service and there will be a price per day per machine with or (usually) without an operator. The crucial factors in negotiations are the condition of the machines which are for hire, the maintenance service and the speed of replacement in case of breakdown. A machine which breaks down and is not repaired or replaced quickly can set off a chain reaction of delays which may cause substantial losses.

Most of the selling in this industry is done by telephone and is in response to telephone enquiries. Contracts are written and exchanged but the 'deal' is often done verbally on the telephone. Salesmen or salesgirls needs to have an up-to-the-minute 'product knowledge' of the kind of machines which are available, their condition, the time taken to deliver them to the site, the service and replacement facilities and, of course, the price. Buyers of plant hire service will want all this information over the telephone and some may want the machine(s) on site within twenty-four hours.

Equipment

Industry is a substantial purchaser of equipment. The term includes tools (generally hand tools), protective clothing and apparati. Some of the purchases such as clothing may be bought on contract; other items are often bought as required. The salesman of such items is often handicapped by lack of knowledge of the 'buying pattern'. The salesman who sells consumable items generally has an accurate idea of his customers' buying cycles. They will order, more or less, every week, every month, or at some fairly regular interval. Since the majority of equipment purchases are made as required, the salesman has difficulty in timing his visits to coincide with favourable buying times. In this situation it is apposite to ask, 'How long does it take to wear out a hammer?'

Some equipment salesmen regularly distribute reply-paid calling cards in the hope that buyers will remember them and at least post the card so that a personal call can be made at an opportune time; alternatively they make regular telephone calls to ask whether the buyer needs anything.

Spare Parts and Consumable Items

The two categories of spare parts and consumable items tend to overlap. A printer using type has to replace it as it becomes worn and the imprint blurs. The letter 'e' wears out quicker than the letter 'z' and, whilst type is bought with this consideration in mind it is, nevertheless, a factor to be considered when re-ordering. Fan belts and driving belts on machines also tend to need frequent replacement. The salesman should try to advise his customers when they buy original equipment of their likely needs of spare parts. Some machinery suppliers make up a spare parts kit which is supplied with the original machinery. It is often of particular importance when selling in the export market. In many developing countries, spare parts are almost non-existent and machines can be out of action for want of a simple component. Local ingenuity is often employed to manufacture substitutes, which may work but are usually merely 'stop-gaps'.

Consumable items are considered here as products which are consumed during the manufacturing process other than as the raw materials used to make the product. They will include such products as lubricating oils and fluids on metal working machinery, cleaning materials, office stationery and the general miscellania required in any organization.

The salesman's task is usually to ascertain the buying cycle and then to time his visits accordingly. However, he needs to assess carefully the potential value of his customer and to allocate his time in proportion to the importance of his customer.

The Industrial Salesman's Main Tasks

It is difficult to give specific guidance on how an industrial salesman should tackle his job. Industrial selling is individualistic and most industries have developed sales techniques, methods and habits which suit them. Many industries have special terms and nomenclatures.

A newcomer to the field should be prepared for a long 'apprenticeship' of on-the-job training. As a first principle, he must study his buyer's needs and the practices within the industry. But in addition he must be watchful to observe trends and changes which may affect future sales relations. Technological developments have altered many industrial methods and these, in turn, have affected the suppliers. Products may need to be modified, other industrial sectors need to be explored and the salesman must be constantly on the alert to monitor current industrial practices and trading patterns and to try to foresee future opportunities.

In industrial selling, product knowledge is essential. No matter what kind of product he is selling, the industrial salesman must be able to give his customer 'on the spot' satisfaction. It is realized that an industrial salesman rarely has the technical competence to give a complete answer to all questions but he should have the knowledge and authority to know when to call upon technical support and to supply it. Also, just as important as customer knowledge today is what is termed 'application knowledge'; this includes some knowledge of how the product can best be applied to suit the customer's requirements.

In some situations, the industrial salesman will also be responsible for negotiating the financial arrangements but it is normal for him to be given training and instruction in the subject.

Industrial selling is a challenging field. Most salesmen engaged in it find the work personally satisfying and, because of the responsibilities which they have to shoulder, it is usually financially rewarding although this must vary from company to company.

10   Career Prospects

It is not many years ago that a salesman's career prospects, in the hierarchic order, were limited to promotion to area sales manager or sales supervisor and perhaps to sales manager when the latter position was mainly concerned with personal selling. One of the main reasons for the limited prospects available to salesmen was that the difference between the personal skills of a salesmen and those required for a manager was considerable and few salesmen were able to bridge the gap.

For example, a salesman rarely has to manage anyone but himself and thus has few opportunities to develop the skills necessary to manage other people. A manager, on the other hand, is almost invariably responsible for leading and controlling some staff. In his day-to-day work, he gives instructions and must do so in an unambiguous manner which will encourage staff to make their best efforts. He must also control the staff and see that the work is done.

Fortunately for the salesman, the marketing function has developed considerably both in concept and organization. Marketing is now regarded in many commercial and industrial organizations as a key function upon which most other functions of the organization depend.

Activities Within the Scope of Marketing

The activities which may come within the scope of marketing include:
1 *Marketing research*
    research into consumer needs
    research into product acceptability
    research into trade and industrial demands, including prices and
    terms
    research into packaging
    research into distribution
    research into competitive marketing and sales activities
    research into competitive publicity
    household and trade audits
    motivation research
    statistical method
    the study, collection, collation and analysis of statistics
    research into future demand
    demand analysis
    economic, industrial and commercial forecasting

2 Distribution

selection and organization of distribution channels
establishment and maintenance of depots
supervision of agents
stock control
operation of transport
shipping and forwarding
storage and packaging

3 Sales

delineation of territories
selection and training of salesmen
supervision of salesmen
sales records, sales statistics
sales correspondence
sales forecasting
sales expense control
sales incentives
samples

4 Publicity

media research
media selection
copy policy
liaison with advertising agents
monitoring of competitive publicity (guard books)
control and verification of publicity
measurement of results
sales promotion
public relations
consumer and trade relations
merchandising
stock control of publicity material
organization of publicity personnel
exhibitions, fairs, seminars
print buying (brochures etc.)

In addition, there is the formulation of marketing, research, distribution, sales and publicity policies, the preparation of departmental budgets and the control of expenditure.

The objectives, purview and organization of the marketing function vary considerably between different enterprises. For example, mail order houses and engineering machine shops have little in common as far as their application of marketing is concerned. An enterprise will organize its marketing function according to its needs. One enterprise may employ hundreds of salesmen but another with the same or even larger turnover may employ none. In the latter case, designs and estimates may be submitted as tenders and presented by a project team of technologists. Nevertheless, it is helpful to show the more conventional infrastructure of the marketing function, as in Figure 10.1.

Figure 10.1 The Marketing Function

Sales Promotion may be sufficiently important to justify a separate department or it may be under the aegis of Publicity or Sales. The same kind of situation may apply to Technical Service.

The scope of marketing in a large organization is considerable. The salesman who wishes to advance his career should take a conscious decision about his own strengths and weaknesses and should assess them in relation to the range of activities available in his organization. Having reviewed the situation, he should ask frankly for a position within his own organization which will broaden his knowledge and experience.

Practical experience is of great value in developing a career but the saying, 'the most practical approach is by correct theory,' should not be forgotten. Many salesmen have been able to bridge the gap between salesman and manager by preparing themselves with courses of study. There are courses available at universities, colleges of higher and further education, colleges of technology, and by correspondence. Fuller information can be obtained from the Chartered Institute of Marketing.

Salesmen wishing to advance their career prospects often pose the question, 'Is it necessary, not only to change the kind of job, but to change the employer as well in order to gain wider experience?' Obviously, there is no general answer to such a question and each case should be decided on its merits. But the salesman who wishes to widen his knowledge and experience must learn to profit from whatever opportunities arise. Changes made within the same company may enhance career prospects there at the expense of widening overall experience. Changes made from one company to another usually enlarge the individual's personal experience but there is always an element of risk in a new environment.

To acquire a more balanced marketing background, most salesmen would benefit from experience in a marketing activity which is totally different from the work of salesmen. Marketing research, for example, requires detachment, objectivity, and an analytical approach, whereas selling is often concerned with the establishment of personal relations and the use of arguments to persuade, sometimes by emotional, irrational appeals as well as by rational arguments. A salesman coming into contact with the 'world of marketing research' cannot fail to notice the wide difference between the personal qualities of researchers and salesmen. Recognition and acknowledgement of the differences is one of the first steps to broadening a salesman's outlook.

Basic Subjects to Study

The salesman wishing to equip himself for promotion must acquire a wider knowledge. While there is no limit to the breadth of study which a salesman can undertake, most salesmen will find it practical to concentrate their studies on subjects which they can reasonably hope to master and to practise competently at some later date.

The choice of subjects is individual and each salesmen should select those for which he feels an aptitude. If, however, he wishes to progress and to acquire professional qualifications he should enquire about the Institute of Marketing's Certificate and Diploma – these will be discussed later. There are some subjects which are almost mandatory for anyone wishing to achieve a managerial position in marketing. These key subjects are Business Organisation, Elements of Statistics, Economics, Legal Aspects of Marketing, Behavioural Aspects of Marketing, and Financial and Management Accounting. A brief background to each of these subjects is given below.

Business Organization

A knowledge of how businesses are organized and managed is an asset to a manager. He can more easily appreciate the problems which arise when decisions are not executed effectively. Also, knowing and understanding how business organizations function enables the manager to transmit decisions and instructions in such a way that they will be clearly understood, which will improve the chances of the instructions being carried out accurately and speedily. Similarly, he is better able to understand the likely impact of his salesmen upon the businesses of his customers.

Elements of Statistics

A deep knowledge of statistics is not necessary but a manager must have an understanding of statistical method and thus be able to appreciate the strengths and weaknesses of the statistical analyses which are presented to him. He should understand how statistics can be collected and collated, the margins of error, the principles of sampling and the dangers of using statistics for a purpose other than that for which they were compiled. An understanding of statistical method usually helps to create a healthy scepticism of exaggerated claims and also develops a more balanced assessment of data.

Economics

Some knowledge of how supply and demand operate is essential for sales staff, particularly the need to match production to the requirements of consumption.

The Legal Aspects of Marketing

Salesmen benefit from, and managers must have, a working knowledge of commercial law. The Acts of Parliament quoted in Chapter 2 give an indication of the various legal requirements which are mandatory in commerce. The legal framework for commercial activity has changed considerably since the second World War and many practices which were legal prior to this period are now quite clearly illegal. The laws of a country usually reflect the social and moral beliefs of its society and the general attitude towards commerce has changed dramatically during the period 1945-1980.

Behavioural Aspects of Marketing

An understanding of some of the factors affecting customer behaviour is vital. A study of the subject gives some introduction to what the behavioural sciences can provide in identifying attitudes, behaviour and motivation among the company's customers.

Financial and Management Accounting

All potential managers need to have an understanding of accounting practice. They will be called upon to prepare budgets and to be responsible for controlling the expenditure of their departments. A knowledge of cost accountancy is also useful. Most marketing managers either decide upon or contribute to the price fixing decisions and prepare promotional schemes. A proposal for a promotional scheme would need to show the costs, the anticipated turnover to be gained, the break-even point and the anticipated extra profit.

Managers within the marketing function are not expected to set up accounting systems but must understand the significance of direct and indirect costs, of fixed and variable expenses, of the contribution to overhead expenses and the benefits and disadvantages of marginal costing.

This aspect of management is of particular importance when a salesman wishes to take a greater responsibility. In most sales organizations, the salesman is preoccupied with turnover and many incentive schemes for salesmen are 'turnover linked'. Such schemes are simple to understand and easy to operate. The salesman can usually calculate his commission earnings easily. But management is concerned with profit and many schemes which are launched to boost sales often end by increasing turnover but reducing the profit ratio. The cost of getting the extra sales has been disproportionate to the profit earned.

The subjects mentioned above are included in Parts I and II of the Certificate Course of the Chartered Institute of Marketing. (The CIM is located at Moor Hall, Cookham, Maidenhead, Berkshire SL6 9QH)

Marketing Qualifications

The career prospects open to a salesman will be enhanced by the possession of a marketing qualification. Some salesmen already have university degrees and a post graduate course in Marketing or the Chartered.Institute of Marketing's Diploma are practical acquisitions which can be used as stepping stones to advancement.

The majority of salesmen, however, are not graduates and many are married with families and cannot, therefore, take time off to study full time. They are obliged to pursue part-time studies while they go about the serious business of earning a living and supporting a family. The salesman should decide which branch of marketing has the greatest appeal to him and is likely to offer him both an interesting and a rewarding career. The Chartered Institute of Marketing offers two qualifications, namely, Certificate in Marketing Studies and the Diploma in Marketing.

Certificate in Marketing Studies

This is awarded for successful completion of the Certificate Course, which is made up of Parts I and II.

Part I

    Fundamentals of Marketing
    Economics of Marketing
    Business Organization
    Elements of Statistics

Part II

    Practice of Marketing
    Legal Aspects of Marketing
    Behavioural Aspects of Marketing
    Financial and Management Accounting

These subjects give a sound body of general background knowledge of marketing.

The Diploma in Marketing

The Diploma is awarded to candidates who complete the examination successfully, and have certain minimum practical experience. The syllabus is composed of four papers which are:

Marketing Management (Planning and Control)
Marketing Management (Organization and Communication)
International Aspects of Marketing
Marketing Management (Analysis and Decision)

Fuller details of the syllabi for both qualifications are available from the Chartered Institute of Marketing.

In addition to the qualifications available from the Chartered Institute of Marketing, there are other professional organizations which offer diplomas of a managerial calibre. They are the Market Research Society and the Communications, Advertising and Marketing Education Foundation (CAM). Both organizations deal with their own specialized subjects and both are based in London.

Executive Appointments in Selling

The salesman seeking advancement may not always have a clear idea of the possible opportunities. Moreover, duties, responsibilities and titles can vary enormously from one organization to another. For example, the sales manager of a company in the mail order business may be responsible for a turnover of several million pounds sterling, but yet not have a single salesman. His equivalent in a company selling fast-moving consumer goods through the distributive trades may have the same turnover and have a few hundred salesmen. Both may be called sales managers. Below are titles of some of the executive appointments which occur in selling, together with a brief description of the kind of duties which they entail.

Sales Supervisor, Sales Team Leader, Senior Salesman, Senior Representative

These are titles which may be given either to an individual operating on his own or to someone who is responsible for a small team. Such titles usually imply a supervisory function in the same sector which is the *raison d'être* for the team. There are many companies whose products have a wide use in many different sectors and it is common practice to organize the sales force on a sectoral basis, e.g. a sales force which sells to the automobile industry whilst a separate sales force will deal with the furniture industry.

With consumer goods, sales teams may be organized in a similar manner with part of the sales force specializing in retail contacts while another part is responsible for wholesalers and/or multiples. The sales force may be divided according to trade classification and a salesman may call on one trade only whilst his colleagues deal with other trades. Each industry and company develops the kind of organization which is best suited to its needs. The duties of sales supervisors etc., when they have a team to lead, can include the following:

initial selection of salesmen (short listing)
leading and training members of the team
directing prospection for new business
quota and target setting (in conjunction with Head Office)
journey planning
expense control
customer contact
periodic reports.

This kind of appointment is one which concentrates on the field operation and the executive usually operates from his own home.

Branch Manager, Area Manager, Regional Manager, Depot Manager

These titles imply a territorial connotation and are usually used in companies and organizations where the sales force is organized geographically. The pithy phrase 'one man, one patch,' describes this kind of organization. Several 'patches' or territories will come under the control of a branch, area, regional or depot manager. There is usually but not always an office for the manager and there may be a showroom or depot.

The duties are similar to those of the previous group but, being organized on a geographical basis, there is likely to be greater responsibility for budgets and profitability. The duties can include:

initial selection of salesmen (short listing)
leading and training members of the team
preparation of budget for branch office, showroom and/or depots
quota and target setting (in conjunction with Head Office)
supervision of stock control and inventories, branch etc.
supervision of maintenance and service of vehicles
direction of prospection for new business
organization of area or regional conferences
journey planning
expense control
customer contact
periodic reports.

For the salesman who takes his first step into management, this is a valuable introduction because he is getting his management experience 'in the field' in familiar surroundings. There is also likely to be a more informal relationship between the staff and the manager.

Field Sales Manager, Sales Operations Manager, Divisional Sales Manager

The title is usually field sales manager and the incumbent is normally located at Head Office. He is responsible for the field operation of the national sales force or the sales division. The division may be constituted on a sectoral or a product basis. If the sales force is large, these executives will usually operate through one of the two previous groups of executives and will direct and co-ordinate their activities. His duties can include:

> development and implementation of recruitment and training policies
> development and implementation of prospection policies
> contribution to the development of sales policy
> co-ordination and supervision of branch etc. budgets and expenditure
> quota and target setting for branches/areas/regions
> leadership and direction of national sales campaigns
> territory/branch/area/region delineation
> development and implementation of sales campaigns and incentive schemes
> customer contact with house accounts
> periodic reports including recommendations for promotion.

The field sales manager must work closely with the sales manager. His role is confined to the field sales operation and is mainly concerned with motivating his subordinates and through them improving the performance of the salesmen.

Sales Promotion Manager

The sales promotion manager is usually responsible to the national sales manager but may report to the field sales manager. In some organizations, sales promotion may be controlled by the advertising department but the hierarchic order will be similar. Sometimes the sales promotion manager has his own staff to implement schemes; on other occasions the schemes may be implemented by the sales force. In either case, the sales promotion work must be closely coordinated with the sales force otherwise it will lose its impact and be less effective. The sales promotion manager's duties can include:

> preparation of promotional budget in cooperation with the sales manager and/or field sales manager
> preparation of sales promotion schemes
> implementation of sales promotion schemes
> accountability and reports on the results of individual schemes
> selection, training and supervision of specialist promotional staff

and/or training of the company's salesmen in promotional techniques

The work of a sales promotion manager usually demands a 'personality.' Anyone embarking on such a career should have an extrovert personality and a penchant for the lively, quick changing ambiance of the promotional world.

Sales Training Manager

The sales training manager is obviously concerned with sales training but he may also be involved in the selection and interviewing of salesmen and in preparing their job descriptions. Training is usually divided into two sections; initial training and continuous or refresher training. The duties of a sales training manager may include:

preparing salesmen's job description
interviewing and selection of salesmen
identification of training need
preparation of training programmes
selection and training of trainers
preparation and acquisition of training aids:
(i) equipment
(ii) material
development of training evaluation techniques
supervising and participating in training
preparation of reports on trainees.

The sales training manager has an important role in helping to create and maintain an efficient sales force. Not only can he make a major contribution to improving the efficiency of a sales force but also, more important, he can boost and maintain high morale among the salesmen.

National Accounts Manager, House Accounts Manager, Special Accounts Manager

Although the title of manager is almost invariably given to the holder of this kind of appointment, he may operate alone and the title is given as a status symbol. However, if the business composing this category justifies the staff, the manager may control a small team. The nature of the work is customer contact with large and/or important accounts or accounts requiring special attention. The latter could include customers who are doing experimental work which uses the company's products. The duties of this executive are likely to be:

cultivation of good customer relations
feed-back of information (this is often a very important duty as large/special customers are frequently trend setters)

price negotiation
negotiations of joint promotions
negotiation of licences, sales concessions, 'own-name' brands
co-ordination of team members.

The function of a national accounts manager, by whatever title he is named, is that of a skilled, experienced sales negotiator who is responsible for handling many of his company's key accounts. His role as manager of a team is usually secondary. In any case, the members of the team will have been chosen for the same qualities which he possesses, namely superior skills in sales negotiation and ability to cultivate good customer relations. Such personnel usually operate better as individuals and find controls and close direction irksome. The team, therefore, is likely to operate with a very light control and the maximum personal initiative. The one very important managerial function when there is a team is to ensure good coordination. It can readily be appreciated that a team empowered to negotiate as individuals could cause anarchy if their price negotiations are not carefully coordinated. The team members often communicate by telephone daily so that all members are currently informed of the state and level of each other's negotiations.

Sales Office Manager

The sales office manager can and should be an important part of the sales impact. A good sales office manager is a morale booster to the sales force. Salesmen remote from Head office are prone, like all other people away from their homes or bases, to feel cut off and alone. Without dramatizing the situation, they can be prey to unnecessary fears and anxieties. A cheque which arrives late, a query unanswered, or a summons, without explanation, to report to Head office can all be causes of tension. The sales office manager who understands these fears can do much to eliminate them and can contribute both to the improved performance of the sales force and the well-being of the salesmen. The general responsibilities of this post will probably include:

general office correspondence
administration of the sales office and, perhaps, accounts
contribution to preparation of the budget and implementation of
    budgetary control
quotations and estimates
sales records and statistics of salesmen's performance
expense control
consumer and customer relations
order control

administration and control of vehicles

control of stocks of sales aids (may be done by the advertising department)

preparation of price lists.

The salesmen who has worked with a good sales office manager will have been fortunate enough to have learnt some of the art of management first hand. If the salesman's first steps into management are in association with such an executive he will obtain a good management 'grounding'.

Sales Manager, Assistant Sales Manager

These two appointments are considered together, as the assistant is usually the understudy and perhaps heir apparent to the sales manager. The sales manager is likely to delegate some duties to the assistant but the choice will almost certainly be based on personal and individual reasons. It will depend upon the personal relations between the two executives and their individual strengths and weaknesses. The main preoccupations of a sales manager are likely to be:

preparation and implementation of sales policy

preparation and implementation of sales budget including the sales forecast

leading and directing the sales force (the 'sales force' may be travelling salesmen, telephone sales girls etc.)

monitoring the performance of the sales force

overall responsibility for the morale and training of the sales force

responsibility for sales development, e.g.

(i) contribution to new and existing product development

(ii) development of improved sales techniques

overall responsibility for sales office, branches/depots under his control

organizing sales conferences.

The extent to which the sales manager can delegate will depend upon the size of the organization and the resources available. The duties of the assistant sales manager may be any part of those of the sales manager but they may also include parts of those specified for other sales executives.

Special characteristics of sales appointments

All appointments within the sales element of marketing have one quality in common; leadership. The individual salesman needs to develop this quality in a special sense by leading his customers towards the buying decision. But it is in executive positions at all levels from branch manager to sales manager that leadership needs to be developed as the dominant characteristic.

Sales executives have to develop the power to influence and to motivate their customers and their own sales staff. A good sales manager should have that quality of leadership which will both inspire and encourage his staff to achieve and maintain high performance standards.

Executive Appointments in Planning, Publicity and Research

Apart from the opportunities for advancement in the selling field, there is a wide variety of appointments in other elements of the marketing function. These include the planning and organization of sales campaigns, publicity, advertising, and marketing research. These appointments require a different set of skills from salesmanship but the salesman who wishes to advance should try to experience an appointment outside the sales element.

The main executive appointments in the other elements of Marketing are set out below.

Sales Planners, Sales Engineers

The sales planner is concerned with the planning of the sales organization, revisions to the organization and the operational planning of sales campaigns and sales tests. The title of sales engineer is not often encountered except in its traditional meaning and, with two possible interpretations, there can be confusion. The traditional meaning was almost self-explanatory and was supplied to a salesman who was also a qualified engineer or perhaps a salesman who had practical engineering experience. In either case, he was employed as a salesman to sell engineering products to engineers. The meaning of the title when employed within the marketing function is quite different.

The sales engineer in marketing is a sales planner who uses some engineering techniques. An example of the application of engineering techniques is the use of work study. The compact book, 'Work Study applied to the Sales Force,' written by J.O. Shaughnessy and published by the British Institute of Management is an admirable example of the transfer of technology between disiplines. The duties of sales planners and sales engineers can be:

job analysis of salesmen's work
delineation of territories
allocation of call values (in conjunction with field personnel)
planning sales campaigns and tests by estimating the 'work' content
preparation of sales manuals and campaign portfolios
design of documents, report forms, customer record cards order
    forms (in conjunction with accountant's department)
journey planning and journey cycle periods

The appointment of sales planners and sales engineers is not widespread but is likely to grow. Changes in trading patterns and methods have stimulated many companies to make changes in the structure of their sales forces and in the sizes and boundaries of salesmen's territories. Some idea of the planning involved and the work of sales planners/engineers can be gauged by examining the list of factors which should be considered before or when changing territory boundaries. They include:

number of active customers
number of potential customers
method(s) of distribution of the product(s)
location of customers within the territory
value of turnover of existing customers
estimate of value of turnover of potential customers
size and importance of customers
ease or difficulty in making a sale
service to be provided at each call and desirable frequency of call
the advantages/disadvantages of a balanced mixture of trade
number of people to be seen at each call
different levels of contact, e.g. director or storeman
identifiable boundaries
equality of opportunity for salesmen, if desirable
availability of supplies/goods to sell
limitations by agreement (some customers may be agents with sole selling rights in a defined area)
available transport facilities for salesmen
the advantages/disadvantages of an even coverage (some products are sold on a fixed journey cycle)
economics of representation

Similarly, when sales campaigns or new products are launched it would be the sales planner or engineer who prepared the operational plan. A typical example could be a new product launch where it would be desirable for all salesmen to break their journey cycles and make immediate contact with their most important customers. Breaking journey cycles will involve extra travelling and re-tracing the routes when the normal journey cycle is resumed.

It is the sales planner/engineer who estimates the time necessary to carry out the operation, evaluates the 'lost' time against the benefits to be gained and who estimates and subsequently calculates the distribution (percentage of stockists) of the new product. This latter is one of the key actions in any campaign which has advertising support. If the advertising 'breaks' before an adequate distribution is achieved, potential buyers will be unable to buy the product and may accept a competitive substitute. The fuller background to the work of the sales planner/engineer is given because it is a developing field and the function is not yet widely understood. This type of appointment is usually made in organizations with large, well-organized, efficient sales forces where the personal sales impact is linked to a carefully planned journey cycle.

Brand/Product Manager

Brand or product managers were first appointed in the fast-moving consumer goods industry. They evolved from a situation in which the sales of single brands reached a level sufficient to justify very large capital investment in production facilities. No businessman likes to have 'all his eggs in one basket'. Diversification is obviously one method of reducing risks but, at the same time, manufacturers wished to protect, to maintain and to promote the single brand which had proved so successful. The brand or product manager was appointed with the sole objective of concentrating his marketing skill on a single product. His duties will vary from company to company but whilst his activities are single-minded and concentrate on the one brand, he rarely has control of the supporting services. The brand/product manager will have to draw on the services of his company's market research, advertising, sales promotion, and sales departments. Priorities and budgets will be decided at a higher level.

The duties of a brand manager will include:

preparation, in conjunction with the market research department, of plans to monitor competitive and own brand sales, consumer preferences, publicity and package appeal;
preparation of promotional schemes for his product;
monitoring and evaluating promotional schemes;
preparing development plans for the brand and making forecasts.

In a large company, there are likely to be several brand managers and each will be making demands upon the company's resources. The development plans and forecasts are likely to be an important factor when claims upon the resources are made.

Marketing Research Appointments

Most companies use the services of specialized marketing research agencies. Even large companies which have a market research department rarely do field investigations. The department's activities are usually divided between commissioning and monitoring marketing researches, carried out on their behalf by specialized agencies, and desk research.

For field investigations by personal interviewers or by post the tasks will include:

preparation of the questionnaire
pilot testing the questionnaire
decisions on composition of the sample

demanding tenders from specialized agencies
choice of agency
monitoring the work of the agency
presentation of the specialized agency's report to company
    executives with recommendations.

Desk research will be concerned with the examination, collection and presentation of published statistics, the perusal of trade, technical and scientific publications, and the preparation and presentation of commercial, industrial, and economic intelligence.

Staff employed in marketing research departments and specialized agencies usually have a university degree or equivalent qualification in statistics, economics, social sciences or kindred subjects. The qualifications of staff employed on desk research are generally less exacting, as most of them work under the supervision of an experienced and qualified researcher.

Advertising Appointments

The situation is analogous to that of marketing research in that almost all companies engaged in advertising use the services of advertising agencies. Many companies commonly employ several agencies at the same time and each agency will be responsible for a product or a group of products. It has been known for two agencies to handle the same product for one company but each had clearly delineated responsibilities.

The advertising department in a company will be responsible for:

recommending the size of the advertising appropriation in
    conjunction with the advertising agency(s)
recommending overall publicity policy
recommending media policy
monitoring advertisements placed and checking copy
checking expenses
measuring results of campaigns
print buying – brochures

A formal qualification is not common among advertising personnel. Most people engaged in advertising have learnt their 'craft' by practising it.

Personal Career Plan

An ambitious man should consciously plan his career. He should decide upon his goals and how he intends to achieve them. It may not always be possible to achieve everything that is planned but the planning itself gives purpose and encouragement to the effort. Moreover, where there is a plan, the planner automatically thinks of alternatives when adjustments have to be made.

The salesman can plan his preferred choice of posts and their duration with his long term objectives in mind. It is as well to remember that when changing jobs he will usually have to complete an application form and this will probably include a list of previous employers. First interviews are often given on the basis of the information shown on the application form and too many changes within a short period of time may create an impression of an unstable candidate.

When changing posts to gain experience, a period of two to three years is usually necessary in each job in order to acquire the experience and have the opportunity to apply it practically. The salesman should remember that a completed application form can show, by recording his previous employment, his step-by-step progression to greater responsibility.

The career prospects for salesmen have expanded considerably. There has been a general acceptance in industry and commerce that job-candidates with broad experience are likely to be more adaptable and competent. Changes of employment are more frequent and employers are more open minded in their attitudes towards prospective candidates.

The various Acts of Parliament dealing with Marketing, particularly the sales element, have changed the working environment of salesmen and have made it more professional by eliminating some undesirable practices. The step from salesman to manager is no longer considered to be an insurmountable obstacle. As a result, the calibre of salesmen has improved and this is recognized by the increased recruitment of salesmen into management.

The salesman who is intent upon self-advancement may find it helpful to have three thoughts in mind. These are:

1 Sales are associated with revenue and profit, in short he starts in a personal up-market position.
2 The good salesman, by nature an optimist, recognizes obstacles and objections as stepping stones which, when well-reconnoitred and exploited, will accelerate progress towards his goal.
3 The quality of enthusiasm is the most important personal attribute and it is highly contagious. The enthusiast not only persuades other people to his way of thinking but gets personal pleasure and satisfaction from it. Anyone who applies himself seriously to the profession of salesmanship can provide himself with a rewarding occupation as well as the stepping stones to higher management.

It is hoped that having reached the end of this small book, those readers who are either salesmen or are contemplating a sales career will have been encouraged to seek ways and means of self-development and to find the way to a better and more rewarding career.

Bibliography

Attwood, C., *The Sales Representative's Handbook* (Business Books, 2nd edition 1971)

Bender, J.F., *How to Sell Well; The Art and Science of Professional Salesmanship* (McGraw Hill 1971)

Blake, R.R. and Mouton, J.R., *Grid for Sales Excellence: Benchmarks for Effective Salesmanship* (McGraw Hill 1970)

British Institute of Management, *Sales Training in Industry* (BIM 1957)

Dibba, O. and Pereira, F., *Promoting Sales* (International Labour Office 1976)

Goldmann, H., *How to Win Customers* (Staples 1973)

Hall, G., *Better Sales through Human Cybernetics* (Human Cybernetics Trust 1974)

Knights, C., *Techniques of Salesmanship* (Pitman, 4th edition 1966)

Lapp, C.I., *Training and Supervising Salesmen* (Prentice Hall 1960)

Lidstone, J., *Training Salesmen on the Job* (Gower Press 1975)

Markaham, V., *Effective Industrial Selling* (Allen and Unwin 1970)

Mepham, J., *How to Buy and Sell; A Negotiator's Handbook* (David and Charles 1976)

Monoghan, M.W., *Accounting for Salesmen* (Business Books 1970)

O'Shaughnessy, J., *Work Study applied to the Sales Force* (BIM 1965)

Sales Consultants, *Organizing the Salesman's Time* (Sales Consultants Ltd, 4th edition 1970)

Tack, A., *How to Train Yourself to Succeed in Selling* (World Work 1964)

Williams, S.A., *Salesmanship* (Teach Yourself Books 1967)

Accounting, financial management, 140, 141, 142
Activities within the scope of marketing, 137-140
  distribution, 138
  marketing research, 137
  publicity, 138
  sales, 138
Acts of Parliament
  see Investigation into distributive requirements, 42
Adaptability of product, 40, 41
Added value, 126
Advertising, 11, 28, 33, 38, 109, 113
Advertising appointments, 152
After sales service (and service), 36, 110, 114
Analysis of competitive products, prices and methods, 37-42
Analysis of main buying interests and motives, 77-85
Appearance of product, 40, 41
Appearance of salesman, 17, 63, 92
Approach to sales interview, 13, 59, 63-5, 69, 73
Area manager, 144
Assistant sales manager, 148

Bad debts, 13
Basic subjects to study, 140-2
  behavioural aspects of marketing, 140, 141, 142
  business organization, 140, 142
  economics, 140, 141, 142
  elements of statistics, 140, 141, 142
  financial, management accounting, 140, 141, 142
  legal aspects of marketing, 140, 141, 142
  see also Institute of Marketing, 139, 142
Behavioural aspects of marketing, 140, 141, 142
Branch manager, 144
Brand manager, 151
Breaking bulk, 121
Bulk packaging, techniques of selling, 129-31
Business organization, 140, 142

Buyer's main interests, analysis of
  see Analysis of main buying interests and motives, 77-85
Buyer's moods, interpretation,
  see Interpretation of buyer's moods, 74-7
Buyers, types
  see Interpretation of buyer's moods, 74-7

Call report, 112
Call values, 49-50
Calls, factors governing frequency, 47-50
  early closing days, 48
  frequency desired by buyers, 48
  number of people to be seen at each call, 49
  rate of stock turn of goods, 48
  size and importance of customer, 47
  stock levels held by customer, 48
  time for prospection, 49
Career plan, 152
Census of Distribution report, 110
Certificate in Marketing studies, 140, 142
Chambers of Commerce, 57
Change parts, techniques of selling, 135
Character of salesman, 11, 21
Chartered Institute of Marketing, 13, 139, 142
  definition of marketing, 13
Classification and credit rating codes, 116
Classified telephone directory, 56
Clearance and premium offers, reporting, 107-8
Closing the sale, 13, 59, 69-73
Codes, use of in reports and records, 116
Collection of accounts, 13, 14
Company liability for complaints, 101
Company policies, reporting reaction, 108-9
Comparative analysis, *see* Competition